I0562345

FAITH, DOUBT, and LISTENING

Endorsements

Roger has the ability to link faith, doubt, relationship, and deep spiritual/psychological insights into relatively brief essays that allow me to explore how and what I think and feel about the world. I find him accessible and down to earth. He is willing to use his brokenness, often with funny and touching anecdotes, to help make my brokenness more acceptable.

—**Gus Jordan, PhD**, Director of Health and Counseling Services, Middlebury College

Roger Marum, you are the "reluctant disciple" whose spirituality is deep and inspiring. Your written thoughts are a continual stimulus to my faith, taking me in new and unknown directions with amazing results. You lead me to consider aspects of my otherwise pedestrian life that are fresh. You keep me alive and on the edge with your occasional explorations. I thank you for your ministry of challenging my orthodoxy and enlivening my faith.

—**The Rev. Bill Lane Doulos**, Founder Jubilee Homes, Author of *Hearts on Fire: The Evolution of an Urban Church*

Reading Roger Marum's spiritual essays always leaves me thinking beyond the scope of his own words into large questions such as where do I stand in relationship to God, how can I be a better friend, how deep is my faith and who was/is Jesus? Roger fearlessly takes the reader into places that he has traveled in his search for truth, leading the way with an open heart, and encouraging the reader with humor, raw emotion, and vulnerability.

—**Jo Anne Kurman**, Singer, *Hometown Beauty Queen* (album), author *Dreams for Sale: Poems and Lyrics*

Doctor Roger Marum is an interesting and effective storyteller. His stories wrestle with real-life issues. The stories are often situations with which we can identify.

Often, they reveal things which we may have been thinking but haven't been able to articulate. He is honest, vulnerable, and transparent. People identify with stories. We recognize something of ourselves in stories told by others. His writings have helped us laugh, maybe cry, practice personal reflection, and have greater empathy in relating with others. Reading his work will take you through all these experiences and bring a smile to your face.

—**Dr. Alan Forsman**, Coauthor of *Crescendo: An Ascent to Vital Living*

FAITH, DOUBT, and LISTENING

LESSONS LEARNED
BY A RELUCTANT DISCIPLE

ROGER A. MARUM, PHD

ELK LAKE PUBLISHING INC

PUBLISHING THE POSITIVE
Plymouth, Massachusetts

Copyright Notice

Faith, Doubt and Listening: Lessons Learned by a Reluctant Disciple

First edition. Copyright © 2022 by Roger Marum. The information contained in this book is the intellectual property of Roger Marum and is governed by United States and International copyright laws. All rights reserved. No part of this publication, either text or image, may be used for any purpose other than personal use. Therefore, reproduction, modification, storage in a retrieval system, or retransmission, in any form or by any means, electronic, mechanical, or otherwise, for reasons other than personal use, except for brief quotations for reviews or articles and promotions, is strictly prohibited without prior written permission by the publisher.

Unless otherwise indicated, all Scripture quotations in this publication are from The Holy Bible, New International Version® NIV®. Copyright © 1973 1978 1984 2011 by Biblica, Inc.®

Scripture quotations marked MSG are taken from *THE MESSAGE*. Copyright © 1993, 2002, 2018 by Eugene H. Peterson. Used by permission of NavPress.

Cover and Interior Design: Derinda Babcock
Editor(s): Mary White Johnson, Judy Hagey, Deb Haggerty

PUBLISHED BY: Elk Lake Publishing, Inc., 35 Dogwood Drive, Plymouth, MA 02360, 2022

Library Cataloging Data

Names: Marum, Roger (Roger Marum)

Faith, Doubt, and Listening: Lessons Learned by a Reluctant Disciple/ Marum, Roger

274 p. 23cm × 15cm (9in × 6 in.)

Identifiers: ISBN-13: 978-1-64949-470-2 (paperback) | 978-1-64949-471-9 (trade paperback) | 978-1-64949-472-6 (e-book)

Key Words: Reluctant Disciple; Searching for God; Waiting in Silence; The Great Mystery; Assurance; Hope; Holy Grace

Library of Congress Control Number: 2022931007 Nonfiction

For the Friday Morning Men's Group at LCPC,
La Cañada, California

Table of Contents

AUTHOR'S NOTE

Walter Wellesley "Red" Smith, Pulitzer Prize winning journalist, when asked if writing a daily column was difficult, reportedly replied: "Why, no. You simply sit down at the typewriter, open your veins, and bleed."[1] Though I had indulged my muse for two decades by dabbling in sporadic writing, mostly fiction, and attending workshops such as the Iowa Summer Writing Festival and the Bread Loaf Writers' Conference, those forays into the writing life had been avocational and hobby-like.

Five years ago, I was approached by a writer to coauthor a book, a memoir, about her struggles with depression, and the treatment interventions which helped her cope with the dark mood swings. The author wanted a clinician who believed a spiritual practice—involving meditation, prayer, and a belief in God, or a Higher Power—could add value as a treatment option. As part of our collaboration, I was encouraged to create a blog in order to build a broader platform for the book. The idea of establishing and writing on a personal website had never occurred to me, so it was with some resistance and more than a dose of reluctance that I plunged into the online world of blogging. And with some advice from those more tech-savvy than I, *Your Reluctant Disciple* (*www.yourreluctantdisciple.com*) was born.

This new commitment embraced a seriousness akin to the one I had with regard to practicing psychotherapy. As eager as I was to write, sitting at the computer, opening a vein, and bleeding onto the screen challenged and exhausted me before I had written the first sentence. The naysaying voice in my head, always a presence to be reckoned with, seemed shriller and more persistent as I ventured into the online life of blogging.

Determined, in spite of doubts about being able to stay the course, let alone whether I had anything to say or the ability to write it, I struggled to come up with an idea for the first piece. The memory of a Catholic church's message board stating "Closed for the Season" came to mind. I'd passed by the Hyannis church on the return trip from Cape Cod the previous autumn, and smiled as I wondered if God shut down and went home with the tourists when summer segued into fall. The random memory had resurfaced on an early morning January commute to my Middlebury office as I approached a similar message board in front of a snow-covered Baptist church. Their announcement declared, "Whoever's Praying for Snow, Please Stop!" that subsequently became the title of the first piece I published on the website in February of 2015.

Equally random thoughts have often been the impetus for pieces I've written during the last five years. Those short essays, now numbering one hundred twenty-eight, have been reflections on my spiritual and psychological journey. Though each has been written honestly, my goal has been the process of becoming more honest, more transparent, and digging deeper.

Faith, Doubt and Listening: Lessons Learned by a Reluctant Disciple is a compilation of the spiritual pieces culled from the website. The journey has been one of seeking truths about God that involve questioning and doubting the tenets of my faith, and wrestling with how my faith resonates with a real world too often in chaos and conflict, a world gone cattywampus—a state not unlike my soul's well-being at times when God feels elusive and absent.

My spiritual explorations did not begin this way. I was born into and raised by evangelical Christian parents, who infused my young life with biblical concepts I found limiting and exclusive. The message they preached was any belief outside the dogma of being "born again" invited eternal damnation to a fiery hell.

This belief system, orthodox in substance, also extended to exclusive views in other human venues. Religious expressions other than evangelical Christianity were earmarked by the devil. Republicans were virtuous—the New York Yankees and Boston Celtics likewise. Classical music was God's chosn form of musical expression. Democrats were the devil's handmaidens, sports teams other than the chosen ones were tainted, and rock 'n roll and jazz were used by the devil to corrupt souls.

I rebelled, rejecting the tidy and sanitized version of how their secular and spiritual worlds existed. I came to believe if God existed, then God had to be more inclusive than the one espoused in my parents' Christian faith. As a preteen, I began questioning and doubting these beliefs, and since open discussion was thought to be unnecessary, if not also of the devil, I closeted my doubts and tried to conform, but the internal unrest and searching for truth persisted. The passionate questioning persisted into adulthood.

However unsettling the serious struggles with faith and belief continued to be, and however unwanted the God of my childhood was, the presence of The Unknown and Great Mystery seemed a constant companion. I pursued college and graduate studies placing me in stimulating academic environments in which the biblical truths my upbringing espoused were affirmed *and* challenged. The quest for answers persisted in waves, often in the form of God-embracing epiphanies, as well as dark periods of abject loneliness riddled with feelings of abandonment by the God whose existence I questioned.

This collection of essays is a peek into my journey, one offering sustenance even as it is fraught with doubts and questions. I am passionate about the quest and believe the uncertainty embedded in faith is a foundational part of belief. Doubts and questions, however disconcerting, have revitalized my faith. There must be a degree of uncertainty when the finite attempts connection with the Infinite.

Theologian Paul Tillich believed doubt "... is an element of faith," and its embrace involves "daring courage" and risk.[2] These pieces are written with those words repeated over and over in my mind, and more often than not they have provided solace to my quivering soul. I know I am not alone on this journey, and hope you, the reader, find something of your own journey in my words.

Roger A. Marum, PhD

October 27, 2020

ACKNOWLEDGMENTS

I am grateful to the loved ones and friends who have encouraged and supported me by reading and commenting on pieces I've written. Though writing is a solitary undertaking, I've never felt alone thanks to them.

I'm thankful to the staff at Elk Lake Publishing for welcoming me into their family of authors. To Derinda Babcock for her work as the cover artist, Mary W. Johnson, the editor who kept me smiling with her sidebar comments, Judy Hagey, managing editor-nonfiction, for her review, and Deb Haggerty, publisher and editor-in-chief, for giving me the opportunity to make my dream come true.

Nikoletta Gjoni used her design skills and social media savvy to make my website and blog posts come alive. Emily Williamson of Williamson Literary has worked with me as an agent, web designer, and editor, and in each role has been tireless in her efforts to bring this book to fruition. Herta B. Feely, of Chrysalis Editorial, has been with me from the beginning. The editorial skills she brought to the project have been indispensable, her stalwart support and encouragement dispelling my doubts while gently pushing me forward.

—PART 1—

LISTENING FOR GOD WHILE FILLED WITH DOUBT

CHAPTER 1

A Surprise Gift

It happens everywhere—in the office or in a deli, in my dreams or in a conversation, even while exercising—you name the setting and I'm quite certain I'll be looking for the God of my childhood. On the third Sunday of Advent in 2015, something special occurred while sitting at the front of the nave in Trinity Episcopal Church in Shelburne, Vermont. This is my chosen place of worship, and though I'm an infrequent attendee, it is where I go when life's darkness hovers and seeps into my soul. That Sunday morning was such a time. It motivated me to get into my car for the ten-minute drive to the nineteenth-century church where I hoped to find solace.

The parish, without a permanent rector for two years, had offered the position to a priest from Massachusetts, who along with his family accepted the call to be the new rector. I'd met him briefly at a monthly men's breakfast and decided then that in addition to seeking God's assistance in lifting the veil of sadness from my soul, I would check him out.

I used to sit in a pew, but several years ago chose the more private alcove where my free-associative form of worship—I don't follow the liturgy, sing the hymns, or do responsive recitations—would go unnoticed. I do scribblings, bow my head, close my eyes, or look around at the stained-glassed windows while others diligently adhere to the liturgical form of worship.

I look for God.

At one point in the service, and I can't remember where the congregants were in the liturgy or what my spiritual or earthly thoughts had been, I looked down at my hands. I was seated, legs apart with the backs of my hands resting on my inner thighs. My hands were cupped with only the fingertips of all ten curled fingers touching. The space between my facing palms provided an unobstructed view to my sockless feet and shoes—it was a warm December day.

I sat motionless, as if transfixed, looking toward the floor.

There was nothing special about my hands other than they were mine. I kept them in place but looked into the nave where other worshippers were reciting a responsive reading, the last line of which was, "Glory to the Father, and to the Son, and to the Holy Ghost"—words I'd said many times—but not today. I returned, with bowed head, to my hands.

Then it occurred to me—here I was, in church, holding my hands in exactly the same position my father had done. When I was three or four, seated in a front pew between my father and mother, nothing captured my attention as much as he did. I'd look at his face, then down to his big hands, and I'd reach over and insert my hand into the space created by his cupped palms. I don't recall he ever looked at me while opening and closing his hands around mine, but I do remember how filled with surprise and joy I was every time I withdrew and then reinserted my hand.

The paper and crayon I'd been given to keep me occupied at the start of the service couldn't compete with the fascination I had for the game we repeated each Sunday morning at the Norwegian United Methodist Church in Brooklyn. I smiled again that morning and allowed the memory of those Sunday services to bring light into my darkness.

My father was very certain about God's existence and the possibility of a personal relationship with him—a loving God. My own faith is fractured by my frequent disbelief and tested by life-shattering events, by the cruelty and brutality existent in the world. That said, I found inspiration in the memory of my father and the new rector's sermon. For a time, the darkness enveloping my soul lifted.

There is something palpable about my father's love for the young child I was when he entertained me during those services. The Old and New Testament narratives about God and Jesus's love are not as palpably real to me as my father's hands and the love they conveyed while playing a simple game of hand hide-and-seek.

I attend church to find comfort and seek relief from life's chaos. I also enjoy the fellowship of other parishioners. I'd like to believe God and I connect, and I experience God's comfort, while I sit quietly in my chair at church and know it as well as I know and remember the warmth, strength, and love of my fun-loving father in that pew many years ago.

December 2015

CHAPTER 2

Moses, the Burning Bush, and the Ants

What struck me while barbecuing the garlic and lemon chicken thighs wasn't the allure of grilling odors and sizzling sounds, but the burning bush ten feet away—its winged branches full of lush green leaves that in three months' time would turn a bright red fall color.

Moses wasn't grilling chicken when he came upon the famous burning bush, as told in Exodus, but he did have a revelation. God wanted him to lead the Israelites from their captors in Egypt. In spite of his doubt and reluctance—"I am not eloquent [but] slow of speech and tongue ... please send someone else"—God convinced him he was the man for the job (Exodus 3:11).

My burning bush was visible through the smoke of the grill, and wasn't aflame, nor did I hear the voice of God. My grilling utensil didn't turn into a snake, and my hand remained free of the leprous sores that Moses experienced as God gave him proof he was who he said he was—"I am who I am."

I do share a kinship of doubt and reluctance with Moses. If God's voice had spoken to me through the bush's lush green leaves, my response would have been the same: "Not me—send someone quicker in speech and tongue, someone more eloquent than I."

Though I experience this doubt about the existence of God on a daily basis, a recent memorial service for a close friend's father brought the issue front and center for me. I was asked to give a reading of the twenty-third Psalm—"The Lord is my shepherd, I shall not want; he maketh me to lie down in green pastures"—a song celebrating fearlessness, contentment, comfort, goodness, and love while being still and restored in God's presence.

On each side of the stage at the front of the church a video screen featured a still image of Caravaggio's painting, *The Incredulity of Saint Thomas*. As in the painting's title, it is incredulity Moses may have felt. Thomas certainly did, and I do with regularity.

I didn't feel fearless, content, or comforted by the Psalmist's poem, which I silently rehearsed ("Even though I walk through the valley of the shadow of death, I fear no evil"), as I focused on Thomas's extended right hand, which reached to probe Jesus's wound.

Pastor Craig, in the worship service preceding the memorial, had referred to Caravaggio's masterpiece, which depicts Thomas's unbelief. He also quoted Frederick Buechner's statement: "Whether your faith is that there is a God or that there is not a God, if you don't have any doubts, you are either kidding yourself or asleep—doubts are the ants in the pants of faith. They keep it awake and moving."[1]

I suffered a similar restlessness while sitting in the third pew awaiting my designated time to take the stage and read the beloved Psalm. When the time came, I stepped up to the lectern, passing the Caravaggio painting and bearing my doubt with me. The recitation of David's words was well received by the family and congregants gathered to celebrate a loved one's life, reinforcing a feeling of hope of God's existence, and, more importantly, knowing their dear departed relative was in good hands.

One week later, while tending to Sunday's dinner on the barbecue, and admiring the spring lushness of the burning bush in our backyard, I revisited Moses's experience at Mt. Horeb. Through the painting and words of Caravaggio and Buechner, my own journey of doubting, questioning, and reluctance led me to what's possible, including the existence of a caring God.

This may be a fleeting disposition, but there will be more barbecues with accompanying smoke and flame, a burning bush bringing challenging stories to mind, and awakened states to remind me "ants" existed thousands of years ago in the Sinai Peninsula as they do today in North Ferrisburgh, Vermont.

I'm listening, God—help ease my unbelief.

June 2015

CHAPTER 3

SEARCHING FOR A MIRACLE IN A DUSTING OF DOUBT

Daybreak on the fourth Sunday of Advent arrived with temperatures in the mid- to high-twenties and the winter's first snow—a dusting which teased of snowfall to come and spurred the hopes of Vermonters wishing for a white Christmas.

Under other circumstances, in the presence of a snow-bearing nor'easter, for example, I might have resisted attending the eight o'clock worship service, stayed warm by the morning fire, and gradually begun the events of the day. But no storm was in the forecast. My interest in attending church was piqued by the unexpected gift of the memory of my father's hands from the previous Sunday. Maybe there was more awaiting this reluctant disciple—and so I made my way back to Trinity Episcopal Church.

Sand had been scattered on the roads, and though there was little traffic, those who did venture out drove cautiously, I among them. I approach these times of structured worship with anticipation, if not the expectation I will be privy to an epiphany or small miracle. I follow Jesse Jackson's exhortation: "Keep hope alive!" My inevitable experience is a mix of wonderment and disappointment.

When I test my finite senses and rational thinking, I often dismiss the practice of being present in a spiritual moment.

Neither allow room for the presence of the Infinite, such as a longed-for epiphany or a desired miracle—an Advent visitation. The gift of the memory of my father's hands raised my hope even as I questioned whether the fond reminiscence contained any spiritual meaning—an answer to my prayer: "Shed some light in the darkness, please." Nonetheless, I continue the journey of keeping hope alive, anticipating something special will occur. I'm a tough sell, but dogged in my fervent pursuit of a palpable and loving God.

The liturgy for the worship service, the one I rarely follow, became the scratch paper on which I scribbled free-associations or random thoughts for later consideration and, perhaps, spiritual enlightenment. I listened with one ear as the rector delivered the homily, focusing the rest of my attention on my soul's meanderings. Among those associations and thoughts were the incredulity of Jesus's virgin birth to an unwed couple, questions about where truth and myth intersect and faith's role when they do meet, and how imperative faith becomes when considering the story of Advent, which, in short, on four consecutive Sundays, is the anticipation and celebration of Jesus's birth.

Other less intriguing Advent facts were lost to me as I doodled and scribbled, until the rector mentioned Sydney Carter's lyrics to "Lord of the Dance"—a song I'd never heard of. The lyricist wrote of Jesus dancing at creation, then and later in the moon, the stars, and even the sun. He left heaven, was born in Bethlehem, and danced on earth.

The concept of a dancing Jesus captured my imagination.

I imagined Jesus dancing in the open field before the seated hungry men, women, and children he was about to feed. I pictured him swirling around the beached fishing boats as he enticed Peter, Andrew, James, and John to give up their life work to follow him. I conjured up the image of a dancing Jesus as he hip-hopped across the waves of the Sea of Galilee beckoning Peter to join him.

This was a serious and fun-loving guy.

I wanted to get up and dance!

Mary Magdalene couldn't resist the charismatic Jesus, nor he her—it defies comprehension to think they didn't dance. I hope they did.

Songs of praise, liturgical readings, most of the rector's homily, and the recitation of the Nicene Creed took place while my soul warmed to thoughts of Mary, Jesus's mother. Luke, the doctor and author of the third gospel, describes her as the creator of "The Song of Mary," which centuries later would become the inspiration for Bach's *Magnificat*.

My worship that day ended with a smile as I envisioned a loving, musical mother and her precocious son, embracing and dancing.

Just as the dusting of snow precedes the first snowfall, I suspect there will always be a dusting of doubt before the moment when light arrives in my soul, as on this occasion, inspired by visions of a carpenter, prophet, and miracle worker who loved to dance.

December 2015

CHAPTER 4

Now I Lay Me Down to Sleep

The evening ritual of saying a bedtime prayer with my father was always something I looked forward to as a child. We would kneel together at the bedside, elbow to elbow, enjoying this special time together.

One night, when I was four years old, the bedtime prayer was going to be different. Dad had agreed he would be there with me as always, but I would recite the prayer alone.

Anticipating our prayer time, I preceded my father into the bedroom where I stopped at the head of the bed. Dad came in right behind me and, as he did each night, kneeled and rested his elbows on the Norwegian duvet covering the single bed. When I took my place beside him, the one to his left and by the pillow at the head of the bed, joy and excitement made thoughts of solemn prayer difficult. Trying as best I could to be still, I stretched my four-year-old body to reach a spot where my elbows would be next to his. As our arms touched, mine tiny and shaking next to his strong and still forearm, we looked in each other's eyes and grinned. I clung to his every word and movement.

"Are you ready?" he asked with a wink of his eye as we settled in for our bedtime prayer.

Then he leaned toward me and, placing his right index finger to his lips, whispered, "Let's say the prayer quietly tonight."

"Will God hear me if I say the prayer quietly?" I asked, as he caressed my cheek.

He smiled.

"Yes, God hears our prayers even when we whisper, because he knows what's in our hearts."

"How can he?"

"Because he's God," my father replied, then draped his arm around my shoulder and held me tight.

I loved being close to my father, and if he knew about God, then I wished to know God too, and wanted both of them to be proud of me.

"Can I start?" I asked, barely containing my excitement.

He rubbed my back and said, "Remember, softly, so we don't awaken Douglas."

"If I forget a part will you help me?"

"Of course I will, but you'll be fine."

I watched and imitated his every move, the way he folded his hands and bowed his head. Taking a deep breath as he had, I began:

> Now I lay me down to sleep,
> I pray the Lord my Soul to keep
> If I should die before I wake,
> I pray the Lord my Soul to take. ... *Again.*[1]

Many nights, after he'd tucked me in, I lay in the dark, anxious and wondering what *if I should die before I wake* meant. I wanted to wake up in the morning, go to school, play, and be with my friends—I didn't want to die in my sleep. My fears were allayed not by the prayer's request, "I pray the Lord my soul to take," but by the touch and presence of my strong and loving father. If this would be the last time we'd be together, I wondered if God would be like him.

Forty years later, eight friends and family sat around the small breakfast nook table in my parents' home. Off to the side on a simple hospice bed, but close enough to be among us, lay my dying father. The morphine drip in the IV line inserted in his left arm was to ease his pain, caused by the cancer for which he and my mother had prayed to God for a miraculous cure. Those of us gathered around the table shared stories, nibbled at finger food, laughed, and cried, and watched for signs of recognition from him, or indications death had come, and he'd gone to be with his Lord.

His ever-vigilant hospice caregiver, in starched white smock, sat across the room in silence. She occasionally raised her eyes from the book she was reading to watch and listen for signs from her patient. "If we don't hear bowel sounds," she'd earlier announced, holding up the stethoscope now draped around her neck, "we'll know he's passed."

With no premeditation on my part, nor scripted plan, I walked to the kitchen counter, picked up a clean serving dish, filled it with warm water, and draped a fluffy washcloth and hand towel over my shoulder. I carried them the short distance to my father's bedside. His eyes opened as I placed the bowl, cloth, and towel on the tray table next to the plastic cup and straw for which he no longer had any use.

"I'm going to bathe you, Dad," I whispered, "okay?"

He moved his lips but made no sound. Although he'd closed his eyes, I thought he smiled, and as he raised his hand and stroked my bare forearm, a tear rolled down his cheek.

I gently placed my arm beneath his shoulders and began to lift him into a sitting position. He tightened the grip on my forearm, and with a slight rotation of his head motioned for me to come closer. As my ear touched his lips, he murmured, "It's all right. I love you, Son."

Someone, I don't remember who but perhaps my mother or brother, came to help me hold him and remove the hospice "johnny" gown loosely covering his now slender body. I began washing and caressing him with the soothing cloth, and then gently dabbed the warm water from his frail and weary body.

It had been decades since I'd thought about the bedtime prayers my father and I had shared, but as I moved my hand over his naked body, the memory of those times and the prayer returned. The lines "... if I should die before I wake, I pray the Lord my soul to take" were altered, and no longer perplexing to me as I repeatedly said to the Great Mystery— "if he should die before he wakes, I pray you, Lord, his soul to take."

February 2019

CHAPTER 5

LOOKING THROUGH THE WINDOW

There is no consoling or comforting "embrace" for me, no answers either as I look outside at the forest where the bucolic view from my home-office window belies the heaviness weighing on my soul.

Why, God?

I await the answer. Nothing.

I am alone, yet in a community of many.

Autumn is giving way to winter. Once-colorful landscapes turn bleak and barren. The large sentinel pines guarding the replenished woodpile by the forest's edge will soon be covered in white. There's a guilelessness to newly fallen snow that my soul desires—a wonderful childlike yearning of innocent magical foolishness. *Whoosh*, and the bleakness disappears as the darkness gives way to light.

Another mass shooting has occurred, and though picture-postcard Vermont seems far removed from Las Vegas and Sutherland Springs, in truth, the perceived "farness" is a denial of convenience.

These events, so real to the bereaved and traumatized, are off in the distance to me—horrific and unimaginable though they are, they impact my soul when I tap into my own losses. Now I feel others' pain and loss as I relive my own bereaving moments—the one of my mother, for example, though she did not die a violent death at the hands of a gunman.

A particularly poignant memory of her involves her constant making of notes. They appeared in the margins of her Bible, on bill receipts, scraps of paper, index cards, both clean and lightly used paper cocktail napkins—on any available pad or shred of paper within reach—and then she filed them according to a system only she understood. On the morning of August 2, 1990, three days after the death of my father, she placed a note, one she'd written but forgotten to send the previous January, on the placemat next to the cup of coffee I'd soon be sipping. I'd driven from Los Angeles to Sun City, Arizona, to be with her, family, and friends as we made arrangements for my father's memorial service and burial. This morning, she and I were the first to awaken.

After our morning hug, I poured coffee and sat across from her at the small breakfast table where she and my father had hoped to share many more meals.

Her perfect penmanship seemed out of place on the yellowing index card in front of me.

"Roger," she'd written, "thank you so much for the *One Year Bible* you gave us this Christmas. These words of the Psalmist have been a daily source of strength for me."

Then I went on to read the quote to which she referred:

> If I keep my eyes on God, I won't trip over my own feet [or anyone else's].
>
> Look at me and help me!
>
> I'm all alone and in big trouble.
>
> The troubles of my heart have multiplied; free me from my anguish.
>
> Look upon my affliction and my distress, my life of hard labor, then lift this ton of [sadness].
>
> Keep watch over me and keep me out of trouble.
>
> Use all your skill to put me together,
>
> I wait to see your finished product.[1]

We sat in silence. I fiddled with the index card, flipping it over and over, from blank side to her small, perfectly spaced words to blank side again. I questioned if she ever wrestled with the way life unfolds as it does, or if she had complete unquestioning trust in God. With Doris, and my father for that matter, there was no room for discussion because as the Psalm suggests, God would take care of everything, whether on a spiritual plane or in daily life.

"You're welcome," I said.

As an inquisitive youngster and a curious young man with many questions, I could not have conversations or entertain a variety of ideas with the two most important people in my life, because my words would be met with, "It's in God's hands." Which may or may not be true, but I always felt stonewalled and diminished by the answer, and subsequently felt left alone with my concerns.

Even now, I'm still puzzled—here were two intelligent people, one a graduate of Columbia University, the other a former student at Juilliard, with whom simple conversations about God and life events could not be had.

And twenty-seven years later that small index card is again in my hands. I turn it over and over as I did then. My mother's blind faith in a present God annoyed me, but it sustained her. When she died four years ago, I'm certain her last thoughts, if she was having them, would have been of heaven.

It is morning, and as I gaze out into the forest, I welcome the light frost covering the ground. Last night's heaviness, though present, is less suffocating. The questions remain in search of comforting answers, but Shakespeare was right— sleep is the balm of hurt minds.

My father's and mother's deaths were expected. They lived full lives. Unlike the loved ones who grieve the deaths of friends and family resulting from random acts of violence, I had time to prepare. That said, nearby and faraway places where people grieve loss—Newton, New

York City, Charleston, Sutherland Springs, Las Vegas, Paris, Berlin, and Utoya, Norway, among others—are members of the same community of human beings I consider "home." Their questions, loss, and grief are mine too.

John Donne, in *Devotions Upon Emergent Occasions*, knew something about the community of man when he wrote: "No man is an island; every man is a piece of the continent, a part of the main ... any man's death diminishes me, because I am involved in mankind, and therefore never send to know for whom the bell tolls; it tolls for thee."[2]

I shake my head and smile as I think of the wonderful question-free beliefs of my parents. If I ever had any doubt of this, I need only call my brother, who would say, "But it's the truth as they saw it, Roger." Still, sometimes I wish their reluctant disciple son had the same level of faith as they did.

My morning-after view from the window remains the same, and then against the green background of the tall pines, a few flakes of snow appear.

November 2017

−PART 2−

HEARING GOD'S VOICE BEYOND
LIFE'S INCESSANT CHATTER

CHAPTER 6

"LISTEN TO YOURSELF ..."

"Listen to yourself, and in that quietude you might hear the voice of God."[1] Maya Angelou, beloved poet and author, said those words, and I believe her.

I love watching and listening to crows. They are believed to be one of the world's most intelligent animals. They construct and adeptly use tools. They commune and play together—and caw incessantly. Their aerial jousting provides them with exercise and pleasure and, to the bystander viewing their aerobatics, much amusement. They live long monogamous lives—perhaps these prolific black birds are on to something.

Crows also live communally, but when I see them standing or perched alone, they often tilt their heads, a movement I assume is designed to hear or see better, but what if in addition to fine-tuning one of their senses, they are listening to something else? Scientists believe they are keen observers of their surroundings, including human beings. Might they also be reflective, given to tilted-head moments of listening to their inner selves—brief periods when the demands and pleasures of the external world give way to crow-like quietude?

Mark Twain was an astute observer of the human race, but his observations emanated from the study of himself, a practice requiring patience and a shrewd "listening ear."

Though considered to be the "Lincoln of American Literature," he was a complex man whose ability to see beneath pretense, and thereby riotously skewer humankind, had its origins in his self-study. Like the crow, I suspect he often tilted his head to better hear the meanderings of his soul.

I don't know of any reference to a meeting between Freud and Twain, but I'm guessing they would have enjoyed each other's company. Freud believed that introspection aimed at elucidating the dark recesses of one's soul would lead to the good life—one of meaning through work and relationships that make life better for ourselves and others. Like Mark Twain, Sigmund Freud was a prodigious writer, a practice requiring extensive periods of listening to himself, and in that quietude discovered truths about himself that, like his satirist counterpart's, had profound application for humanity.

Maya Angelou believed, "There is no greater agony than being an untold story inside yourself."[2]

Finding a perch, a place, or space of respite wherein the necessary demands of life may be momentarily put aside can be difficult. We may need to do more than tilt our heads this way and that to better take in the voice of God, our singular story, or the narrative of our respective souls.

Maya Angelou, Mark Twain, and Sigmund Freud were acute listeners and observers of themselves, and "wrote themselves empty," but still had more to explore, discover, and write about.

We cannot release or embrace the voice and story unless we stop and listen to ourselves, and even then the cawing may drown out the inner self trying to be heard.

A poet extraordinaire, a brilliant satirist, and a dedicated student of man's soul may guide and encourage us to find a place of quietude, but so too can the crow perched in the Monterrey pine, head tilted, looking back at us, and perhaps reflecting on all things internal and crow-like.

March 2015

CHAPTER 7

A GROWING HUMILITY

St. Teresa of Ávila, a Spanish Carmelite nun, wrote this prayer in the sixteenth-century. She was part of a community of sisters espousing vows of poverty, obedience, and chastity while devoting themselves to serving others. She chose the path of an ascetic, consecrating herself to a life of prayer and contemplation while isolated from the public.

I discovered this prayer on the end-page of the program memorializing and celebrating the 103-year life of a beloved wife, sibling, mother, mother-in-law, grandmother, great-grandmother, and friend. I met her twice, and over the years heard many stories about her—all of which suggested this would not only be her prayer but a way of being in which she fully lived.

This is a petition for divine intercession as well as a request for assistance in the practice of solid psychological principles and common sense.

This is an entreaty having spiritual, psychological, and common-sense value for me as I segue into my seventieth year. It would have been poignant for the younger man I was who believed he had all the answers—not just decades ago, but yesterday as well.

St. Teresa's Prayer:

Lord, thou knowest better than I know myself that I am growing older and will someday be old. Keep me from the fatal habit of thinking I must say something on every subject and on every occasion. Release me from craving to straighten out everybody's affairs. Make me thoughtful but not moody, helpful but not bossy. With my vast stores of wisdom, it seems a pity not to use it all, but thou knowest that I want a few friends at the end.

Keep my mind free from the recital of endless details; give me wings to get to the point. Seal my lips on my aches and pains. They are increasing, and love of rehearsing them is becoming sweeter as the years go by. I dare not ask for grace enough to enjoy the tales of other's pains but help me endure them with patience.

I dare not ask for improved memory, but for a growing humility and a lessening cocksureness when my memory seems to clash with the memories of others. Teach me the glorious lesson that occasionally I may be mistaken. Keep me reasonably sweet; I do not want to be a saint (some of them are so hard to live with), but a sour old person is one of the crowning works of the devil. Give me the ability to see good things in unexpected places, and talents in unexpected people. And, give me, O Lord , the grace to tell them so.

AMEN.

September 2015

CHAPTER 8

IN CAHOOTS

There is no pharmacy in my neighborhood which offers an inoculation against the ravages of inequity, injustice, and racism. No vaccine is available to remedy homelessness, economic hardship, or loss of employment, let alone the loss of life caused by a relentless virus. And the contagious pandemic of uncertainty infecting all of us continues to spike and surge. If I thought otherwise, ever-present masks and taped reminders to social distance would awaken me to our new reality.

My reservoirs are tapped, my taken-for-granted energy almost depleted, and my Job-like patience tested to limits I'd never imagined. Though I remind myself daily we are resilient human beings, my get-up-and-go resources are challenged. Days become weeks, and as I become accustomed to flat-screen relationships in my practice, I miss the depth and nuance of face-to-face gathering.

Yesterday, today, and tomorrow's uncertainty are wearing me out.

Several days ago, I sought respite from my pandemic doldrums in the music of my favorite rock group, The Band. Their fourth album, *Cahoots*, had been languishing unplayed for a year or more while I'd listened to other more popular CDs from them. A Saturday morning trip to recycle and dispose of trash seemed the perfect time to turn up the Volvo's speakers and fill the car's interior with good ol', down-home, rock 'n roll. Songs like "Life is a Carnival," "Where Do We Go From Here?," "Smoke Signal," and "Thinkin' Out Loud," whose titles and lyrics have stirred my soul since first discovering the five-member band in the late '60s, have now become siren calls for alarm.

After getting in line at the recycling site, I turned down the music. I "thought out loud" about the Band's tunes. *Are people sufficiently heeding the distressing "smoke signals" of COVID data and pandemic guidelines? Where do we go from here?* I wondered, because, right now, life is anything but a carnival.

My concerns and questions about life's inequities and injustices, God's presence or absence, and life's purpose and meaning have been intensified. Life in 2020, with its external events impacting all of us, has colluded with internal anxieties to create an ever-present state of apprehension. I believe it to be true for many of us. It is certainly true for me.

Engaging in mindless Netflix shows offers only temporary distraction. My reading habit results are the same. But as I dig deeper to make sense of the chaos, I find respite and solace in the words of cohorts who've become friends, ones who open new and familiar pathways to me. They are the usual suspects I too often relegate to dusty shelves, but their hope-filled messages get a necessary dusting when my desperation becomes suffocating.

Toni Morrison's words from her 1993 Nobel Lecture encourage me to write and journal my thoughts. "We die. That may be the meaning of our lives," she said. "But we do language. That may be the measure of our lives."[1]

Sigmund Freud's belief that we are sustained in life by gratifying relationships, and engagement in "work that helps us and others to have a better life"[2] invites me to be grateful for friends and loved ones and people who invite me into their lives in my psychotherapy practice.

The Franciscan friar William of Occam thought that though multiple valid explanations may apply, it is most likely the simplest that's correct. The cobwebs of overthinking become dismantled when I affirm Occam's razor.

Søren Kierkegaard instills hope in my vulnerable and fragile soul, bolstering my weakened faith when he writes that doubt yearns to believe.

And when I go to the familiar writings of the Psalmist, I find solace and good company in the prayers: "God, God, save me! I'm in over my head, quicksand under me, swamp water over me: I'm going down for the third time. I'm hoarse from calling for help, bleary-eyed from searching the sky for God (Psalm 69:1–3 MSG) ... [but I also believe] ... you have bedded me down in lush meadows, you find me quiet pools to drink from ... you let me catch my breath" (Psalm 23:1–2 MSG).

There is no pharmacy in my neighborhood to inoculate me against the ravages of society's illnesses. However, my cohorts—the writers, poets, and musicians whose works reside nearby on my bookcase shelves—allay my fears. In cahoots with them, I find sustenance and respite from all that afflicts us. Their words feed and nurture me.

October 2020

CHAPTER 9

HE CAME TO HIMSELF

Saint Luke, evangelist and physician, is the only one of the four gospel writers in the New Testament who documents Jesus's confrontation with the Pharisees in which he tells the parable of the prodigal son. The reading of Luke's account was part of the liturgy this past Sunday. I attended the worship service while reminiscing about my deceased father whose 102nd birthday would have been celebrated on March 5, and also reflecting on author Pat Conroy's death the day before. In the parable, the younger son of a wealthy landowner asks for his share of his father's estate. The father complies with his son's request, and the latter moves to a distant country where he squanders his monies and becomes destitute. Neither Jesus nor Luke suggests reasons for the son's request and subsequent lifestyle—although "dissolute living" can be alluring. Was there dysfunction in the family? We are left to wonder, and though that is not the point of the parable, as a clinician I wonder about the father's and son's decisions. The son eventually returns to his family of origin, much to the chagrin of his older brother, where he is embraced and feted with food and drink during a festive community celebration.

I have read and studied Luke's narrative, but on this Sunday the words "he came to himself" drew me into the tale in ways I'd not experienced before. The young son, penniless and starving, found his way into reconciliation with his past and into a renewed life.

Pat Conroy, in his novels *The Great Santini*, *The Lords of Discipline*, and *The Prince of Tides*, used his childhood experiences to shape and inform his characters and their stories. He was the eldest of seven children, and like his siblings, he was subjected to his father's sadistic abuse and incessant ridicule. Writing, though not therapeutic for Pat Conroy, was essential to his understanding of himself. Following the publication of *The Great Santini*, Pat and his father, Donald, found some peace and reconciliation in their relationship.

My father, unlike Donald Conroy, was not brutalizing and sadistic, but he was critical and judgmental, demeaning, and dismissive of me. As I grew older and gained more independence, my father resented not being the center of my world. As a result, like Conroy, I grew up both loving and hating my father and often considered running away.

Brokenness affects many of us and can be handed down from parent to child if left unexplored. We may be born into families in which love's expression becomes intertwined with harmful, if not destructive, communications which mute the loving. My personal life, including broken relationships and divorces, has been a perpetuation of those experiences with added twists of my own.

When on trial, Socrates is said to have stated the unexamined life is not worth living—his choice was death over exile because he believed he would be able to continue unabated questioning and examining in the afterlife. His words are often paraphrased to encourage self-examination through which insight and healthier living might occur.

We know the prodigal son "came to himself" when confronted with the brokenness of his dissolute life. I interpret this to be the result of connecting the messy external world of pig-feeding and squalor to his soul's desire for reconciliation with father and family.

Pat Conroy used his gift for storytelling and skill as a writer to explain his life to himself, and subsequently to discover some peace and reconciliation with his father.

My psychotherapy, while in graduate school and for years afterward, brought healing to my brokenness—a lifelong effort of coming to myself that remains challenging and at times elusive—many years after my father and I reconciled.

Coming to one's self is not for the timid but takes courage, whether you're in a pig sty wanting something more, or putting pen to paper to see yourself more clearly, or immersing yourself in the gentle art of psychotherapy, or being vulnerable to the gifts of grace and forgiveness.

March 2016

CHAPTER 10

THOUGHTS ON A FRENCH WORD

The word *depression*, however commonplace in our lexicon, still retains a sledgehammer effect when I hear it used to indicate a state of being—mine or anyone else's. Aside from its use to describe a well-entrenched, disabling mood disorder, I prefer the French *ennui*, a lighter shading of mood description. It can be subtle and seductive, like a fine Pinot Noir or Cabernet Sauvignon, unlike depression, which may overwhelm the senses like an aged piece of Roquefort. Ennui arrives out of the shadows, offering the possibility of change, whereas depression bludgeons us with hopelessness, a sense change is impossible.

Once again, my meandering mind or soul has latched onto a word which stirs my curiosity and desire to make sense of feelings, moods, and emotions. This time, as is often the case, with respected, albeit unlikely companions—Winston Churchill, Sigmund Freud, Bruno Bettelheim, D. W. Winnicott, Martin Luther, Maya Angelou, and Leonard Cohen—whose writings suggest they're in agreement, that being sad and weary has a place and offers an invitation into what may be possible. "*On we,*" as ennui is pronounced, signals the journeying from shadow into the light of becoming.

The word *ennui,* the French word for boredom or weariness, is a first cousin of *annoy.* Ennui may signify lethargic disappointment, unexpected melancholy, a deflation, or sudden disappearance of zest. I know, because it has done so to me on occasion when colors fade, joy is elusive, and every step I take is annoyingly difficult.

While lying in the dark, doesn't it sound better to have a diagnosis in French—*ennui*—than the English cudgel—*depression*? Tolerating or managing disappointment or sadness in a relationship, or experiencing the despair following an unexpected life event, seems more doable for me when I self-diagnose a spot of ennui rather than a "rough patch" of depression. Languor and lassitude, like their kin, ennui, bring a smile to my face when I say them aloud in the midst of strife.

That smile, however, is easily altered by disruptive and annoying struggles. The chattering of my inner world and the clanging discordant sounds of the outside world both vie for my attention, impact my mood, and unsettle the balance in my life. When confronted by my personal inner hell (and current events sap my resilience), I think of Winston Churchill encouraging the British people to keep going regardless of how dark and bleak circumstances may be.

And as I "keep going," wrestling with spates of ennui, I receive comfort from Freud's belief the purpose of psychoanalysis would, through exploring our sadness, make us become wiser. In D. W. Winnicott's words as paraphrased by my analyst Dr. James O. Laughrun, "We cannot experience what we cannot remember, and we cannot remember what we try to forget." Freud believed in and recommended psychoanalysis (introspection and reflection of one's soul) because it can reveal the connection(s) between our essence and actions and enable us to live fully into our greater humanity.

Bruno Bettelheim states: "The good life, in Freud's view, is one that is full of meaning through the lasting, sustaining, mutually gratifying relations we are able to establish with those we love, and through the satisfaction we derive from knowing that we are engaged in work that helps us and others to have a better life ... and our dark impulses are not allowed to draw us into their chaotic and often destructive orbit."[1] God knows my palpable dark impulses may crave expression, and their denial fosters ironic disappointment and relief.

I'm keeping on, Sir Churchill.

Martin Luther, the sixteenth-century German monk and theologian, knew about ennui before the word existed. He ran afoul of Pope Leo X for his beliefs and was excommunicated from the Catholic Church. I imagine he experienced a spot of ennui prior to declaring his enlightenment, as he wrote: "This life is not righteous, but growth in righteousness; is not health, but healing; not being, but becoming; not rest, but exercise; we are not yet what we shall be, but we are growing toward it; the process is not yet finished, but it is going on; this is not the end, but it is the road; all does not yet gleam in glory, but all is being purified."[2]

Luther's convictions are given a contemporary voice in the words of Maya Angelou:

> I'm working at trying to be a Christian and that's serious business. It's not something where you think, "Oh, I've got it done. I did it all day—hot diggity." The truth is all day long you try to do it, try to be it. And then in the evening, if you're honest and have a little courage, you look at yourself and say, "Hmmm. I only blew it eighty-six times. Not bad." I'm trying to be a Christian. I'm always amazed when people walk up to me and say, "I'm a Christian." I always think, "Already? You've already got it? My goodness, you're fast."[3]

The ennui of life's frustrations, sadness, and pain became her friends. It was the pursuing, the working and trying, not the arriving, that filled her with hope and stoked her faith.

Her recitations of poetry, that unmistakable voice of passion and wisdom, have inspired me in times of sorrow and hopelessness when I succumb to ennui. Though I've never heard Ms. Angelou sing, I can imagine her in a duet with Leonard Cohen performing a paraphrase of his iconic song, *Anthem*, affirming the presence of hope, and striving for light amid brokenness and sadness. Leave your perfect offering at the door and ring all of the bells. Look into the dark for therein is the crack that allows the light to come in:

Ennui is a buoyant word for me, offering hope in the shadows. Depression, however appropriate a diagnostic label under certain conditions, has an end-game finality to it.

There are no solutions, so say the prime minister, psychoanalysts, theologians, and poets, nor is there perfection. However imperfect life may be, fraught with ennui, there is a crack in everything through which the light may emerge to shine on our brokenness and that of the world, and bring illumination to both. Persistent ennui is no match against the strivings for keeping on, learning and self-knowledge, speaking our truths, living a spiritual life, and embracing hope.

November 2018

CHAPTER 11

THE GIFT THAT WON'T GO AWAY

Perseveration ...

This is a good and worthy word which describes a thought process of mine, one I'd like to be rid of.

I've analyzed it to death, sealed it in a tomb, but continue to retrace my steps to the sealed entrance, where inside the word capturing my bedeviling habit—*perseverating*—awaits me.

I perseverate, and then perseverate about perseverating.

It's not crippling or debilitating, but to say the thought process is simply annoying would be to understate its impact.

Have you ever asked yourself a question, come up with an answer, but revisited, clung to, and worked the question ad nauseam even when the answer is reasonable and true?

It's a personal disorder not (yet) found in the diagnostics and statistical manual (DSM-5), the diagnostic bible for mental health professionals, but it is real for me. Merriam-Webster defines perseveration as *the continuation of something (as repetition of a word) usually to an exceptional degree or beyond a desired point*. Some DSM-5 disorders include perseverative thinking and behaviors as symptoms, obsessive-compulsive disorder (OCD) for one.

I resist using some good and useful words because they are too academic or are employed to impress the listener—

algorithm, pedagogy, rubric, and *trope* come to mind. I'd like to excise *perseverate* from my personal dictionary, free my mind and soul of its presence by relegating it to the shelf where the aforementioned words collect dust.

I cannot do it.

Both *perseverate* and *perseverance* come from the Latin root *persist,* but the latter suggests tenacity, singleness of purpose, grit, backbone, and pluck. There's nothing gritty, tenacious, or doggedly courageous about my perseverations.

A priest friend of mine once suggested my doubt and questioning, and I might add perseverating, were God's gift to me.

It's unopened, God. Take it back. Please.

Easter Sunday has come and gone. Jesus's body is gone from the tomb in which it was placed. Resurrection has occurred, Mary weeps, and the disciples don't doubt her tale of the empty tomb, but they doubt Jesus has been resurrected. Perhaps his remains have been stolen, maybe misplaced—who knows—but missing for certain.

The painting on my website, Caravaggio's portrayal of Thomas requiring hands-on proof he is risen, captures my state of being with a personal wrinkle. I'd leave Jesus's presence, knowing how persuasive he was, walk away, wonder, and perseverate about his scarred hands and abdominal wound, thinking (and perseverating) *there's got to be an explanation.* Perhaps I'm hallucinating, or maybe it's a good makeup job, a sleight-of-hand miracle worker, maybe a stunt double. People don't rise from the dead.

When faced with compelling client conflicts, trauma, and struggles, I frequently wonder if I make the best decisions, and lock into wondering beyond what is reasonable. *Do I listen closely enough to my clients? Are the warranted interventions working? Did I miss something?* All good and appropriate considerations, but when the questions persist to the point where their existence becomes annoying and repetitive—I'm perseverating.

In my family of origin, I knew my parents loved me, but I often wondered if I met their expectations for what a good-enough son should be. Praise and affirmation were rarely served around our dinner table. This wondering persists in my personal relationships. *Am I a good friend, partner, spouse?*

On the outside I may appear confident, savvy, perhaps even smart and charming, quick of wit, thoughtful, maybe even wise. Inside, my soul is equally rich in rational and irrational thoughts and feelings which create doubts and questions about the above traits. Some perseverations are trivial (*Did I unplug the coffee pot? Turn off the bathroom light?*) while others are significant (*Was I loving, attentive, and present enough?*)

Ernest Hemingway's words give me hope: "There are some things which cannot be learned quickly, and time, which is all we have, must be paid heavily for their acquiring. They are the very simplest things, and because it takes a man's life to know them, the little new that each man gets from life is very costly, and the only heritage he has to leave."[1]

April 2016

CHAPTER 12

FINDING THE HOLY

Can your senses, any or all of them, detect the presence of the holy?

Mine, reluctant disciple that I am, too frequently miss the signs of its presence even when its voice cries out, "I'm here!"

But on Saturday, June 2, for a short time and for reasons which remain a mystery, I became immersed in the holy.

It turned out to be a picture-postcard afternoon in Vermont. The barn, or sugarhouse—the building where maple sap is boiled and made into maple syrup and maple sugar—provided the setting where an extraordinary local civil servant would be presented with the Colleen Haag Public Service Award. Each year, the recipient is honored by the town of Shelburne for service and dedication to the community.

Driving to Palmer's Sugarhouse, a place I'd never visited, I marveled at the roadside wooden barns and bridges I passed. The beauty of the distant Green Mountains provided backdrop to the countryside where copses of maple and pine trees lined the road. Open pastures flanked the dirt roads and two-lane blacktops on which I drove. The simple, plain-looking barn, the home of the fifty-year-old family sugaring business, sat on a knoll. Weathered and gray on the outside but vibrant and alive on the inside, the sugarhouse reverberated with the sounds of friendly greetings and laughter, fellowship, and community.

People sat either on picnic tables or long wooden benches or stood by the large evaporator in which the sap and water boiled or congregated near displays or clustered around the entrance. It was a standing-room-only crowd of joyful souls, filling the spacious sugarhouse to pay tribute to a man they knew and loved.

Jim Warden, retired police chief and renowned storyteller, had it going on that Saturday just as he had during the thirty years he protected and served the town of Shelburne, Vermont. Affable, grateful, serious, commanding in his presence, and humble before family, friends, and peers, Jim was gracious and impressive as he accepted the award. The chief lived fully in what those present had known him to be during his years of service on the job, and in the roles he took on that went beyond the scope of his duties. He served equally as confidant, counselor, dog trainer (think dog whisperer), and a never-ending source of stories.

Sitting among friends, fellow congregants from the North Ferrisburgh United Methodist Church, and people from Shelburne and surrounding townships, I had come to pay tribute, feel companionship, and celebrate community in the presence of a fine man.

Handwritten menus, posters, and news clippings graced the walls of the barn-like structure while above us in the rafters retired farming and sugaring tools hung. Shelves were adorned with a variety of containers, some iconic and antique, and others tasty—jugs and glass jars filled with maple syrup or maple cream, along with neatly stacked gift boxes of maple sugar and candy ready for sale.

The trip through the peaceful and gorgeous countryside to and from the sugarhouse, the many smiles, greetings, and expressions of affection and gratitude toward Jim—all these combined to create a sense of being part of something grander.

A feeling of welcome and belonging engulfed me, a sensation of ease and unspoken companionship. Love and kindness shone through the smiles, the hugs and handshakes, and the warm greetings of those present in this down-home Vermont gathering.

In the random and mysterious manner by which thoughts often occur to me, I remembered the words of writer Anne Lamott: "I can tell you that what you're looking for is already inside you. You've heard this before, but the holy thing inside you really is that which causes you to seek it. You can't buy it, lease it, rent it, date it, or apply for it."[1]

In the midst of celebratory kinship, a welcome spell of unscripted togetherness occurred between my soul and the familiar and unknown folks around me. I felt a connection to something "beyond," yet tethered to the people, event, and local countryside. I shifted in my seat, tilted my head in puzzlement, but paid attention.

At the time, my thoughts and feelings were private, so I resisted saying anything to Tom or Ted, the friends on either side of me. And then while attending to the kind and humorous anecdotes offered in tribute to Jim, I began to realize what was occurring. As I sat there glaze-eyed, my elbows propped on the red and white checkered, maple-syrup-sticky, plastic tablecloth, I was surrounded by holiness. The great web of life, as Frederick Buechner calls it, was unfolding within and around me, and at its core the presence of the sacred.

It was all quite simple, really, and therefore easily passed over—no bells and whistles, thunderclaps, or lightning bolts to my soul. There was no conscious searching on my part, no "attempt to buy it, lease it, rent it, date it, or apply for it."

It just appeared, the presence of the holy, where it has always been.

June 2018

—PART 3—

Waiting in Silence; God, You Have My Attention

CHAPTER 13

WHEN MY SOUL SPEAKS TO ME

When my soul speaks to me, I listen.
When my soul speaks to me, I listen and ask, God?
When my soul speaks to me, I [try] to listen, regardless of what else is happening.

I wrote these lines on New Year's Eve 2015. They led me to the words of Bruno Bettelheim, a psychoanalyst whose book, *Freud and Man's Soul*, I've read many times, each one giving birth to renewed hope for myself and humankind. The author wrote the book because "the English translations of Freud's writings not only distort some of the central concepts of psychoanalysis but actually make it impossible for the reader to recognize that Freud's ultimate concern was man's soul, the basic element of our common humanity—what it is, how it manifests itself in everything we do and dream."[1]

Nowhere in Freud's prolific writing (manuscripts and correspondence) does he offer a precise definition of what he means by "soul." He does interchange the words *soul* and *psyche*, and states that soul or psyche is what is most valuable to human—humankind's essence, something intangible yet powerful—and in conflict. It is the place from which our passions emanate, and our minds inform and direct us. Various drives compete for dominance and control of our souls. This struggle can bring a richness of healthy emotion and well-being to our lives, but may entail equal measures of befuddlement and clarity, elation and depression, joy and sadness, and through these experiences we find and then reach our soul's deepest meaning.

Back to my listening habit.

I don't make New Year's resolutions because my life tends to be an ongoing series of evolving resolutions involving hopes, dreams, and expectations, an ongoing search for truth and wisdom, and plans for implementing part or all of them. These manifest themselves in relationships, professional practice, habits I embrace—prayer, exercise, meditation, writing, reading—and the one I'm least faithful in doing, care for my soul, a quiet time requiring active listening—focused and open to whatever occurs.

A linear graph would show my mixed results of exhilarating spikes and precipitous drops, and when I don't live fully into the hopes and dreams, the disappointment compounds the frustration of not achieving a steady ascent. When I get slogged down by "stuff," I become impatient, resist sitting quietly and listening attentively, always hoping for insight or God's whispered words, "Roger, I'm missing you."

These are the times when digging deeper becomes tough. There are aspects of who I am that I do not enjoy (and sometimes don't even remember), let alone want to confront, yet these are the foibles or brokenness most in need of exploration, insight, and healing.

My therapist's words came back to me: "We cannot experience what we cannot remember, and we cannot remember what we try to forget."

Freud suggested meaning and the good life come with satisfying and sustaining relationships with those we love, and work which helps us and others to have a better life. His use of the term "soul" has an inexactness to it, but it resonates with me at an emotional level. In my fragile spiritual core, the word *soul* arouses my attention, perks me up, and I declare with anticipation my hope for a romance with my soul.

"Speak to me, soul. I'm listening."

January 2016

CHAPTER 14

BALANCING PENNIES

The consistent back and forth movement and ticking sounds of the metronome were mesmerizing and made me want to leave the piano bench, jump around, and dance. The two pennies carefully placed on my wrists to eliminate extraneous hand movement and keep them steady failed to do so, nor could their presence rein in my five-year-old impulse to fidget. I was not created to be still.

When the coins fell, clinking on the ivory keys or bouncing off the piano bench, any pretense of maternal patience disappeared. I became the object of my mother's withering disapproval and the recipient of a guilt-inducing scolding. On one occasion, I screamed in protest, threatened to throw the pennies down the toilet, and to stick a piece of bubble-gum on the metronome's pendulum. The subsequent outburst from my mother included the dreaded words, *Wait until your father gets home*, which implied a lecture and spanking before dinner.

After months of intense instruction and spotty practice sessions, my mother and father gave up the dream of having their firstborn become a pianist, the master of an instrument they both enjoyed playing. For me it was a Pyrrhic victory. They decided I would be a violinist instead, dismissing my desires to play the trumpet or be a "feast of moving parts," untethered, a dervish of flailing arms and legs pounding and peddling away on a drum set.

"You have a God-given talent to play the violin," my father declared. "It would be the devil's handiwork if you failed to embrace the gift." He would frequently close lectures with frustration and anger, declaring, "Why do you have to do things the hard way?"

Always powerful figures in my family's daily life, God and the devil now became warring combatants not only in how I approached fiddling, but in how I lived my life—even as a youngster. Being a good boy (godly), a dutiful son, often clashed with a stubborn and unyielding desire to have my way (devil-driven). I could be equal parts compliant and rebellious, often accepting praise for the former and condemnation for the latter as equal and affirming measures of who and what I was becoming—blessed and damned. Years later, I learned while on my analyst's couch that this sometimes costly and conundrum-like way of being enabled me to survive.

God became a demanding and insatiable taskmaster, while the devil offered respite and pleasure. When drawn to rebellious and impulsive action (of the devil) I came to expect a humbling comeuppance pie (God-baked) waiting on a menu somewhere. Good-boy efforts, playing by others' rules, seemed to deny my voice and in so doing created suffocating self-doubt. Brazen, although unfulfilling, forays into devilish and risky behaviors became my norm, and though I loved feeling rakish, I despised the emptiness often accompanying my actions. I loathed this conundrum but invited and embraced it nonetheless. Looking in the mirror often stimulated a one-or-the-other wish for life either as a hell-bound reprobate, free of the religious roots with which I'd been raised, or as a heaven-bound saint who lived above reproach and wrong-doing.

Instead of sticking either to the wicked low road or the high sanctified one, I have found a way to "balance the pennies." There are times in life when I play the notes as written in the script and the coins remain in place, a comfortable and assuring way to live. Those days when I go off script, the coins bounce off the keys and clink on the floor, improvisation takes over, and I make mistakes, trusting with time and patience I'll find my way.

When stricken down by the weightiness of self-doubt, I know there's work ahead which will lighten the load, a process I've come to embrace while appreciating the pendulum swings between confidence and self-doubt, angelic and devilish behavior. I know such swings are an inevitable part of my life. I would not experience life as the vibrant yet puzzling journey I have come to expect if I lived it any other way.

Sometimes I want to flush the copper cash of doubt and devilry and the goody-two-shoes offering-plate nickels I discover in my pocket, but I've learned to hold on to them and mindfully see what they can teach me. At these times, reflection, mindfulness, candid conversations with God, and exercise help bring the controlled chaos of the metronome's beat back into focus.

It has been a while since I threw that tantrum by the Steinway & Sons piano, but the gratitude for lessons learned the hard way has endured.

March 2020

CHAPTER 15

PASSING THROUGH CHARYBDIS ON THE WAY TO ADVENT

The wet sheet wrapped itself around my legs, a tangled mess I was too tired to fix. The pillowcase was damp, and no matter what direction I turned the sweat created by dream-filled REM sleep chilled my body head to toe. My hopeless struggles with bedding, exhausting as they were, paled compared to the relentless sound and sight of the word *Charybdis* in my dreams. A clownish carnival barker shouted "Charybdis!" while standing beneath a blinding Broadway marquee declaring opening night of the play *CHARYBDIS*, starring Roger Marum. It was 1:30 on the morning of December 8, the first Saturday of Advent.

Desperate attempts to silence my inner turmoil through prayer failed. My requests became, as they often do, demands and rants about what God needed to fix. Please, I shouted, get us back on track and eliminate chaos, and while you're at it, wipe out my self-absorbing craziness. Where are you? If you're infinite, take care of this and change that, and do it NOW.

Hours passed, and herds of numbered sheep, offered prayers, and meditations with mindful breathing failed to disentangle me from the clinging Egyptian cotton and the troubling dreamscape. When the alarm went off at 6:00, I was relieved the night had come to an end even without the desired rest.

My curiosity about Charybdis, a second cup of coffee, and the instant access of the internet joined together to inform me about the Greek myth of Scylla and Charybdis, two terrifying sea monsters at the Strait of Messina between Sicily and the mainland of Italy. These mythic figures forced seafarers to choose between two evils: Scylla, the six-headed monster, or Charybdis, the devouring whirlpool.

I'd spent the night teetering on the edge of a whirlpool.

Reluctant to shelve my questions about the restless night but committed to attend the 7:30 monthly men's breakfast at the North Ferrisburgh United Methodist Church, I dressed and drove to the meeting. Tangled strands of the messiness of the previous night lingered as Ed, a church member, led a discussion on "waiting," which began with his statement: "A waiting person is someone who is present to the moment, who believes that this moment is *the* moment."

Ironic, I thought as I listened to others among our group of ten share their thoughts on the subject while I continued to wrestle with the previous night's events, including my haranguing God for not taking care of business.

Embracing the silence to listen while waiting is elusive and uncomfortable to my soul as I chatter away and clutter the emptiness so there's little room for the Great Mystery to speak. Writer Debie Thomas gets what too often eludes me: "Silent prayer asks me to believe that God's work has little to do with my consciousness or emotional experience and that what happens in the silence [of waiting] is meant to be mysterious—even to me."[1]

The Old Testament prophet Isaiah prophesied (Isaiah 11:6–9 NIV):

> The wolf will live with the lamb,
> the leopard will lie down with the goat,
> the calf and the lion and the yearling together;
> and a little child will lead them.
> The cow will feed with the bear,
> their young will lie down together,

and the lion will eat straw like the ox.
The infant will play near the cobra's den,
And the young child will put its hand into the viper's nest.
They will neither harm nor destroy
on all my holy mountain,
for the earth will be full of the knowledge of the LORD
as the waters cover the sea.

That's what I wish for the world this Advent season, as well as that which Thoreau and Kipling address when they respectively write about "all good abides with him who waits wisely,"[2] and "if you can wait and not be tired by waiting ..."[3]

Patience in life, let alone in prayer, is foreign to my experience and practice of either. St. John of the Cross writes that the first language of God was and is silence, a thought I can agree with but fail to practice.

Returning home after the breakfast, I sought relief and quiet in my office. Ed's prompts and the thoughts of the others caused me to ask if I could learn to be patient, to embrace waiting in stillness for The Other to speak. I am a reluctant disciple, filled with question and doubt. Is my desire for God wishful thinking? Or do my cluttering rants and incessant laments fill the silence God needs to be heard?

Joseph Campbell wrote: "We must be willing to get rid of the life we have planned, so as to have the life that is waiting for us."[4] Those words make me smile as I read them. Not only have I planned a life, but I script my prayers to fill the space, and fall in love with my words and thoughts, leaving little room for the smiling Mystery to be heard.

There is comfort in the words of Frederick Buechner: "We work and goof off, we love and we dream, we have wonderful times and awful times, are cruelly hurt and hurt others cruelly, get mad and get bored and scared stiff and ache with desire, do all such human things as these, and if our faith (whatever it may be) is not mainly window dressing or a rabbit's foot or fire insurance, it is because it grows out of precisely this kind of human compost."[5]

A night of thrashing added to my human compost pile, and it was my hope this Advent season that out of the mix of ingredients, a new birth may occur. Perhaps a measure of holiness will appear in the silent waiting, and when it does, my Christmas wish for all of us is we'll experience what the white pearl tells Rinkitink in L. Frank Baum's book *The Land of Oz:* "Never question the truth of what you fail to understand, for the world is filled with wonders ...."[6]

December 2018

CHAPTER 16

IT'S MORE THAN A LENTEN PRACTICE

Note: Two essays, "The Meandering Mind of a Reluctant Disciple," *originally posted in April 2016, and* "A Lenten Practice," *March 2018, were combined and updated for this new piece, completed in June 2020. Recent events—the COVID-19 pandemic and ongoing racial injustice, the latter again making headlines with the murder of George Floyd on May 25, 2020—deepened my doubts and questions about God.*

In 2018, Lent, the season of reflection and preparation before the celebration of Easter, began on February 14, Ash Wednesday. The first of two brief readings I had chosen for the day was written by Henri Nouwen in *Bread for the Journey*: "We all have dreams about the perfect life: a life without pain, sadness, conflict, or war. The spiritual challenge is to experience glimpses of this perfect life right in the middle of our many struggles."[1]

That morning as I opened the adult coloring book to pursue my Lenten coloring practice, his words threaded their way through my soul, my thoughts and feelings, known and unknown, conscious and unconscious. I picked from among the dozens of coloring pens in their windowsill mason jars in my home-office waiting area—neon-colored pens, some with glitter, others traditional—all waiting to be chosen to express my artistic muse.

I dreamed of perfection, of coloring within the lines, and then struggled to let go of the craziness and replace those thoughts with acceptance of my outside-the-lines flawed strokes. It was a battle, but I kept coloring, crossing over the lines, breathing, smiling, cursing, and hoping for respite in spite of the inner demand to create a masterpiece. When frustration's vise grip overwhelmed me, I danced—also a Lenten practice I've adopted. I once unwittingly revealed it to the UPS driver as he placed a package on the porch and caught sight of me doing a wild and silly version of the Lindy Hop while circling the island in the kitchen. He smiled and gave me a thumbs-up as I exorcised my demons.

In *Listening to Your Life: Daily Meditations*, Frederick Buechner writes about observing Lent and suggests during this time, "Christians are supposed to ask one way or another what it means to be themselves."[2] His suggestion prompted my own questions as I wondered: *Is there a God? What does it mean to be me? What is the meaning of life? Why am I here?*

Henri and Frederick became daily companions as I colored and danced, read and journaled, sought God and answers, took in new questions while rehashing old ones, colored outside the lines, and on occasion found fleeting stillness amid the restless doubt and questioning.

I try embracing Freud's contention that belief in God, the ultimate loving father, was my human yearning to make sense out of the chaos in the world, the pain, sadness, conflict, and injustices we inflict on others and ourselves. Though his idea made rational sense, it remained an inadequate explanation for the vigor behind both my wrestling with doubt and my joy in the "dance."

The final days of the season of Lent approached. On an early Sunday morning, Palm Sunday to be exact, I drove the short distance to Trinity Episcopal Church in Shelburne, Vermont, to attend a worship service. During the homily, I knew I'd be reminded Jesus's Passion was about to unfold. His entry into Jerusalem, a disappointing time with *his* reluctant disciples, a mock trial, and crucifixion were his destiny. His own people, Jews, and Roman authorities were complicit in bringing about a week of confusion, dashed hopes, broken hearts, and unbearable sadness.

Holy smoke, I thought as I drove through part of Vermont's bucolic Champlain Valley, *can't we skip The Passion and go straight to The Resurrection?*

Remembering Henri Nouwen's words to find a glimpse "... of this perfect life right in the middle of our struggles,"[3] I opened the center console and blindly chose a CD from among the ones stored there, a random act which brought immediate relief. I love music and the feelings artists stir in my soul—The Five Satins, The Platters, Willie Nelson, Miles Davis, Thelonious Monk, Vladimir Horowitz, Jessye Norman, Jussi Bjorling, and Itzhak Perlman, to name a few. I pushed the CD into place and turned up the speakers.

As I reached the crest of the hill north of Mount Philo, Little Caesar & The Romans were singing the doo-wop classic "Those Oldies but Goodies (Remind Me of You)"—a fitting selection given this day.

Doo-wop *a capella* arrangements created on inner city street corners by black and white male and female singers surrounded me. My Volvo rocked and swayed to their harmonizing voices as I trekked through pastures and farmland in the Champlain Valley.

This little Caesar and *his* Romans sang with bravado, snapping their fingers and tapping their feet. I sang along, alternately singing lead well above my register, then dropping my jaw to mimic the deep sounds of the bass.

I love to lip-sync with the harmonizing voices, and wondered if, in happier times, Jesus's followers didn't feel a similar exhilaration in his presence. I've imagined Jesus dancing, perhaps with Mary Magdalene, while the fishermen-disciples snapped their fingers and tapped their feet against the hulls of their beached fishing boats. Saint Peter might have been the lusty bass, Matthew the soaring tenor, Thomas the one providing a rich baritone, Judas creating rhythm by shaking the small bag of tribute pennies tied around his waist, and Mary and Joanna (mother of James) as the incredible backup singers.

I can also picture them on the road, blending voices in heartfelt harmonies, making up lyrics and nonsense syllables of love and loss during breaks between treks across the sweltering countryside and barren landscapes. I wonder what Jesus would have been thinking or planning. Would he stop for prayer, tell a puzzling parable, heal a sick child, comfort an outcast, commit a mind-boggling miracle, gently but firmly confront religious hypocrites, expose ethnic injustice and financial inequities, or just keep dancing down the road?

The Palm Sunday liturgical worship service was a blur to me as I enjoyed thoughts of the coloring book, the meditations I'd read, and the music I'd enjoyed. As the time came for the sacrament of Holy Communion, I realized I'd already been participating in a sumptuous feast. Just as it was in 2016 and 2018, so too is it in 2020. The Great Mystery has been present throughout, in the music of the street, in my fantasies, my lamentations, and my joy.

Neither Nouwen nor Buechner suggest anything other than simply, God is.

June 2020

CHAPTER 17

LOVING, HATING, AND LIVING WELL

I hate you, I thought, with the same five-year-old's passion with which I'd said, "I love you" to her that very morning.

The hateful thought, possibly my first conscious one but certainly not the last in a life of loving and hating, occurred at dinner when my mother insisted I eat the lima beans I'd separated from the rest of the succotash by dispersing them to the side of my plate. Desserts, which my mother created with loving attention, were the reward for suffering through her favorite veggie concoctions. The ostracized inedible lima beans, however tasteless, cold, clammy, sandy, and gritty, were chewed and swallowed. If it weren't for the lovingly made chocolate silk pie my clean plate promised, I'd have vomited on the spot.

Several years later, my father was on the road when, late one night, my mother received the call that my beloved grandmother had died. "I hate God for taking Grandma away," I declared at my mother's bedside when she told me the news. But I didn't stop there. "Daddy hates him too for taking away his mother," I said through my tears. Her cheeks were dry, her lips pursed, and her facial expression a withering scowl as she grabbed my arm and said, "Shame on you. Don't you ever talk about God that way, or think your loving father would ever hate anyone, let alone God!"

As a child, I was encouraged and taught to love, and punished for hateful thoughts or feelings. Love was (in theory) given unconditionally, but in fact it was parceled out, or so it seemed, and hateful thoughts were of the devil and therefore evil. My parents did instill in me the importance of loving and being loved, but however well-intended their efforts, love's expression and acceptance came with conditions—lessons they'd been taught and passed on.

The early lesson was to love the other based on merit, and deny or distance yourself from troublesome (but normal) hateful thoughts and feelings. This was the antithesis, I later learned, of what needs to occur for a healthy life. Giving love without attachment to conditions while learning to accept the other is sound practice. Acknowledging hateful feelings and then finding ways to exercise restraint over their expression is also good practice. Neither had a place in my family. The guilt I felt for hating was a feeling apparently foreign to my parents, and one which made me different from and unacceptable to them. Their response left me puzzled and hurt with no one to bail me out. I was alone.

"I love you" was an expression voiced in greetings and departures, at bedtime, and following mealtime prayers. The phrase, a staple in our family, has always been one with which I'm comfortable saying but not necessarily successful at doing. At the same time, feelings and thoughts driven by anger and hate were closeted, shut away in my soul and mind because having them could only mean there was something wrong with me.

Lord Byron described hatred as a madness in the heart. Mahatma Gandhi stated: "Hate the sin and not the sinner is a [general rule] which, though easy to understand, is rarely practiced."[1] As a child and adult, confronting "madness of the heart" meant acknowledging unpardonable hate, a task for which I was ill prepared, and therefore Gandhi's counsel lay beyond my reach.

Frederick Buechner writes: "To lose yourself in another's arms, or in another's company, or in suffering for all men who suffer, including the ones who inflict suffering upon you—to lose yourself in such ways is to find yourself. Is what it's all about. Is what love is."[2]

His words meant for me to love fully I'd not only have to lose myself in the suffering of others and those who inflict suffering on me, but address my own hidden suffering, the hateful thoughts and feelings, and lose myself in them to then find myself, and love.

In his provocative and insightful collection of lectures, *On Loving, Hating, and Living Well,* Ralph Greenson (I've borrowed his title) writes:

> Sometimes it is necessary to accept misery and injustice and tyranny, but not to like it, and not to accept it blindly. A healthy person is a person who can also rebel, complain, squawk, and fight, and not one who is in line with everyone, and is the same as everyone. The healthy human being is flexible and part of being mature is feeling able to disagree. The psychoanalyst further states: ... how in childhood there is a good mommy and a bad mommy, but mom she is, and how it could be that to feel simultaneous love and hate for the same object is an achievement in development.[3]

Not to oversimplify our complex humanity (because nothing human is ever uncomplicated), but we can be double-minded creatures—a person, according to the Greeks, who is of two minds or souls, or as my hate-love interior world indicated, someone who is a youngster in conflict with himself.

To choke off the unacceptable and extol the acceptable at the former's expense left an imbalance in my inner world, a suffocating state of being. Years of work on my analyst's couch brought life and acceptance to what had before been unpardonable, and legitimacy of the existence of hateful thought and feelings. It brought balance to my soul and helped me from acting on darker feelings in destructive ways, a lifetime's work still in progress.

My parents' love for me and mine for them was never in question, but the brokenness with which they were raised and passed on to me kept us from loving, hating, and living well, or as fully as we were meant to live, a fate I strive to change.

October 2017

−PART 4−

GRASPING FOR AND HOLDING ON TO FAITH

CHAPTER 18

IN TIMES OF TROUBLE

NOTE: The following occurred during the first week of February 2020 and had no connection to the Coronavirus (COVID-19), or at least I believe so, which at the time seemed like an "over there" problem.

"Are you real, and if so, where are you, God?"

"Yes, I'm real, I exist, and I'm here."

That question and real-time pleading, followed by a wished-for imagined response, came after many shameless solicitations during my fevered, sleepless, and vulnerable condition brought about by a viral infection.

In my depleted, flu-like state, the thought occurred to me death would be welcome, and I called out for divine assistance to die, be healed, or at minimum be offered a whispered word of assurance.

The growing pile of used tissues, empty bottle of Robitussin, stack of books I was too miserable to read, and partly consumed gallon of spring water on my nightstand attested to my fragile condition—certainly not a terminal one, but a delirious one from which I desperately wanted relief.

"Take me now," I pleaded. "I can't bear this another hour."

Too ill and exhausted for continued pleading, I lay in the darkness moaning and sniffling, seeking elusive sleep while hoping for relief. When none came, I tried to appreciate my privileged good life and first-world problem. Musings about how fortunate I was compared to millions, if not billions of others, didn't alter or quell my self-absorbed whimpering. Nor did my symptoms lessen—the nagging croupy cough and aching body driving me to the take-me-please frame of mind. Instead my body continued to fail me, and my soul's desperation persisted.

Stripped of control, fragile and vulnerable, my tremulous voice barely above a whisper, I cried, and cried out with unapologetic abandon, "Help me. Where are you?"

The desperation and tear-filled unabashed pleadings, as far as I could determine, brought forth only silence even as daylight arrived. I felt helpless, overwhelmed, suffocating in a colorless world.

I had quarantined myself in the back bedroom to protect other members of the household, but now I felt abandoned by them *and* God.

"Blessed is the one who perseveres under trial" (James 1:12 NIV), words from the Epistle of James, attributed to James, Jesus's brother or to James the Less. I, "Roger the Less," felt no blessedness during my brief but compelling sickness, a trial in which I did not feel like persevering or that I was blessed.

Approximately ninety-six hours later, a first-in-four-days meal—the untoasted half of a cold Thomas's English muffin—in my belly, and looking every bit like the resurrected Lazarus, I shed my "grave clothes" and began waddling into wellness.

My initially cautious gait and unstable movement rapidly evolved into striding with authority, exercising, resuming the work I love, being with people, and renewing the pleasures of the five senses, fully restored and functional. Regaining control of my life brought intimations of my immortality, hints that being vulnerable and fragile, even needy were accepted as collateral symptoms of the flu, to be dismissed as temporary aberrations.

As my strength returned, the thoughts that God had sheltered in place, stayed home and left me, became "Shame on me, because I know better."

Now, more than one month later and removed from my solitary world of sweat-soaked bedding and flannel PJs reeking of illness and body odor, not to mention my shameful, post-illness arrogance, I'm part of a global community struggling to deal with disease and dis-ease as COVID-19 brings sickness and darkness home to us all.

Life is out of control as we're all asked to alter lifestyles in an attempt to stem the onslaught of an insidious virus. We're doing this for ourselves and others. Feeling a familiar vulnerability, the unnerving discomfort of the unknown, I'm working to embrace hope. Though in what, I'm not always certain. Epidemiologists, leaders, and researchers may have answers. Practicing social distancing, sheltering-in-place, and suffering through quarantines may be best practice. My hands are the cleanest they've ever been. More than all of the above it is the promise of the presence of the Great Mystery into which I'll throw my lot.

When I feel boxed in, desperate and lost because control eludes me—always overrated anyway—I often turn to authors for companionship, and James will be one I'll be revisiting. And here's a "friend" from my graduate school days, one whose writings I dismissed in a cavalier manner, but whose words stayed with me in spite of my arrogance. Gustave Fechner, nineteenth-century German philosopher, physicist and psychologist wrote about "healthy faith," and those like me who say we'll believe it when we see it. Though I cannot recall his exact words, this is the gist of it: "You will only believe it when you see it, but you must believe it before you see it."

And so, with his sense and faith I'll peer into the darkness, looking for relief and answers, believing what I cannot see and seeing what I can't fully believe.

Stay well, keep the faith, keep washing your hands, and here are some parting words from Frederick Buechner: "This side of paradise, we are each of us so nearly all the other has. There is darkness beyond our wildest imagining all around us. Among us there is just about enough light to get by."[1]

March 2020

CHAPTER 19

THOUGHTS FOR A SUNDAY: BLUEBERRIES, VAN MORRISON, ROUGH SEAS, AND THE (TEMPORARY) STILLING OF A DOUBTER'S SOUL

The pastor of the church I began attending in the spring of 2017 asked if I would fill in for her on a Sunday in August while she and her husband were on vacation.

When she approached me about taking on this task, she put it as, "Would you be willing to preach while I'm on vacation?" My first thought was *No! I'm a psychologist—we're not supposed to preach, we listen.* Then, feeling like Moses the prophet, leader of the Israelites, standing before the burning bush and confronted by God, I asked, "Why me?"

"You're not Moses," she responded, as if reading my mind, "and I'm most certainly not God." And then she asked, "Why *not* you?"

"I'm new here," I said, "and besides that, preaching is something my loving father did every night at the dinner table, and then there was my bigger-than-life maternal grandfather, a Methodist minister, who scared me when he preached one of his hellfire and brimstone sermons."

"Don't preach, then," she said. "Tell one of your stories about your spiritual journey."

I was beginning to learn what the parishioners of my new church already knew—she would not be denied.

I left the meeting thinking of the Psalmist's prayer: "May these words of my mouth and this meditation of my heart be pleasing in your sight, LORD, my Rock and my Redeemer" (Psalm 19:14 NIV).

I set about the task of coming up with a story or two which would tie in with the Scripture from that Sunday's lectionary. The twin themes of doubt and faith almost instantly sprang to mind, and one of the stories I might use followed close behind.

My fragile faith and bedrock doubt appear at times when I'm least prepared and most vulnerable, and a recent outing at Pelkey's Blueberry Farm, a few miles up the road from the church where we worshipped, provided such a setting. I'd wandered away from my wife and other blueberry pickers and walked down a row of bushes sagging under the weight of plump, glistening blueberries.

It was a beautiful Saturday morning with a breathtaking view to the west—clear skies, a slight breeze, Lake Champlain and the Adirondacks in the distance. And though glad to be taking in the wonder of the succulent blueberry bushes and the distant landscape, I was troubled and unable to put my finger on the source of my consternation.

I began a conversation with God, a daily occurrence for me, often beginning with two questions and a plea: "Where are you?" followed by, "Why do you sleep when I need you the most?" and finally, "Help!"

"I'm here, Roger," said the voice in my head, "right where I've always said I'd be, next to you—I'm beside you, the one for whom you've been searching. Look into and then beyond the obvious. I'm in the dark and the light, the openings and empty places, all the spaces where I fill the gaps. Rest in my presence."

We left the farm and drove home with two bags totaling more than twenty pounds of lush blueberries. Strangely, I felt lighter, as though a weight had been lifted from my shoulders. Along an open portion of Greenbush Road, cornfields on both sides, I recalled the Psalmist's words: "You, LORD, keep my lamp burning; my God turns my darkness into light. With your help I can advance against a troop; with my God I can scale a wall" (Psalm 18:28–29 NIV).

This story, I hoped, would resonate with fellow congregants who also questioned the strength of their faith, had doubts, and wondered if God heard their prayers. With this in mind, the Scripture I chose for the day was Mark 4:35–41 (MSG):

> "Late that day he said to them, 'Let's go across to the other side.' They took him in the boat as he was. Other boats came along. A huge storm came up. Waves poured into the boat, threatening to sink it. And Jesus was in the stern, head on a pillow, sleeping! They roused him, saying, 'Teacher, is it nothing to you that we're going down?' Awake now, he told the wind to pipe down and said to the sea, 'Quiet! Settle down!' The wind ran out of breath; the sea became smooth as glass. Jesus reprimanded the disciples: 'Why are you such cowards? Don't you have any faith at all?' They were in absolute awe, staggered. 'Who is this, anyway?' they asked. 'Wind and sea at his beck and call!'

And so, with some trepidation I planned to expose myself. Like the disciples in the storm-tossed boat on the Sea of Galilee, I get anxious, have doubts, have my faith shaken, and then am surprised when God's voice proclaims, "Quiet! Be still! Why are you so afraid? Do you still have no faith?"

The second tale of my challenged faith occurred on a March night earlier that year, a night I lay in bed unable to put to rest unwanted and persistent questions about my faith. Though a full moon illuminated the south-facing bedroom where I lay awake, a darkness filled my mind and soul. Like the fearful disciples in the boat, I was anxious and doubting.

My alarm was set for 5:30. I tossed and turned, wrestled with unwanted thoughts and feelings, distractions which appear only in the silent dark of the night. I recited a mantra of mine—

"Jesus, son of the living God, have mercy on me, a sinner"—
then added, "help me sleep, please!" Nothing occurred.

At around two in the morning, the runaway thoughts
and feelings were replaced by the music of Jean Sibelius's
"Finlandia." Over and over again, my sleep was interrupted
by the orchestral sounds of a symphony being played
inside my head against my will. Finally, the alarm went off
as scheduled, and while having my usual morning cup of
coffee, I realized I was feeling surprisingly rested. I got in my
Volvo, turned on a Van Morrison CD, and headed south on
Route 7 for my first office appointment while singing along
to "Moondance."

As I drove through New Haven Junction, an unexpected
desire for quiet came over me. I stopped singing, turned off
the CD player, and exited the junction in stillness. As I looked
out of the side window at the cloud-topped Green Mountains
to the east, I began singing the lyrics from the hymn "Be
Still My Soul" to the tune of "Finlandia." The hum of the
tires on the pavement faded as my voice grew stronger, and I
robustly sang the first verse over and over until I reached my
office in the Marble Works.

I sat quietly, ignition off, breathless and bewildered in
equal measure. God had spoken in the dark of night, but I
hadn't listened. The orchestral sounds at two in the morning
were his answer to my prayer. "Be still," God had whispered,
and in spite of my closed ears he'd given me rest.

The church service proceeded as planned. The two stories
of a current and present reluctant disciple resonated with
members of the congregation. During the post-service coffee
hour, many shared vignettes from their own lives in which
doubt and challenged faith had left them anxious. They
too expressed surprise by the Great Mystery appearing in
unexpected ways to still the "seas" and bring calm to their
restless souls. Listening and being still serves me well and
bolsters my faith for the inevitable time ahead when doubt
will fill my soul.

October 2017

CHAPTER 20

How Betting and Faith Shape My Life

What is it grounding me in all facets of my life? I've asked that question for decades, tried on different answers, but the question always resurfaces. One answer, and it's simple: "serial betting"—and faith seem to have been my practice—trusting in my own abilities, coupled to a shaky faith in God. Though ignorance is my constant companion and I bet on outcomes even when I don't know I'm betting, it is faith, not wishful thinking, that guides me along the way.

When I was six, my friends and I frequently hiked into the woods abutting our suburban neighborhood. To get to our frequent destinations, Duck Pond and Sugar Pond, we had to cross a flowing brook whose mucky banks were overgrown with skunk cabbage plants. If broken, the plants released the pungent odor of their namesake.

"Betcha can't," Bruce taunted on one such occasion.

In my neighborhood, a bet, dare, or challenge required a response. I surveyed what lay before me, turned to Bruce, and smiled.

"Bet I can," I replied, with the bravado only a six-year-old can pretend to possess.

I guessed, given a running start, I could leap over the streaming water, smelly plants, and clear the squishy mud, but I wasn't certain. Pride and my status on the block were at stake—kid stuff. Bruce's offer of his purple lollipop was a bonus.

That day in the woods, with Bruce and my buddies, I thought I understood the challenge. Leap over the plants, muck, and water, and be celebrated. End up in the drink, and we'd have a laugh, my mother notwithstanding. All that was accurate and age-appropriate for a six-year-old determined to prove his mettle. I was, however, more ignorant than knowing, betting on the outcome and unconsciously placing myself in the hands of faith. That was the real challenge, something which didn't occur to me then, but does now as I reflect on choices and decisions I've made over time.

None of us standing by the creek that day were brazen and foolish—scraped, bruised, and battered by risky-but-fun behaviors, yes, but we all relished the challenge and opportunity to prove ourselves in front of our peers. Like most first-grade boys, we pushed and prodded each other into feats of daring. Whether we succeeded or failed, a guileless faith in ourselves seemed inherently present, something most of us lose with the onset of maturity.

The skunk cabbage test of character and courage came to mind as I was thinking about how often daily life forces us to wager, and the role faith plays in our actions and decisions. In my six-year-old mind, I objectively decided I could make it across the brook. But I was actually betting on a desired outcome, trusting in faith and hope more than in hard data. Even if I'd cleared this natural obstacle many times—hard data—this attempt would still be a leap of faith.

We all bet, often wagering with our very lives. Think about boarding any vehicle of transport, whether you or someone else is in control, or eating a meal in a restaurant. You place yourself at risk by putting your health and safety into someone else's hands—a pilot, train conductor, a chef, the restaurant manager.

Too often, I downplay the part faith and trust have in decisions I make, and arrogantly believe *I know* is the guiding operative phrase for my choices.

I'm not as smart as I like to think I am. There is, however, one exception.

The smartest stance I've taken is knowing ignorance is my constant companion. I bet on outcomes all the time, and faith, whether I've acknowledged it or not, is what drives my decisions and actions. I've come to embrace a world of "un-knowing" rather than one of fact-gathering and knowing. Living fully means embracing uncertainty, discarding the illusion I'm in control with my satchel full of facts and knowledge. It is relieving to accept my "betting life," anchored in faith. It's also scary with its endless possibilities.

My faith is fragile and frequently challenged. At such times, I resort to the comfortable "old ways" wherein I believed I was in charge, managing and controlling choices and decisions. Being informed is important, but when it dismisses the role uncertainty and faith play in life, being informed is a false posture.

I've returned to the woods near my home of origin. Though its course has been altered over the years, the brook still flows, and where skunk cabbage once thrived, weeds and barren ground have replaced the smelly plant. Where a running start was once necessary to cross, I now simply step over the brook, but the element of faith remains.

I don't know for certain if God exists. I can't be certain a client who seeks my assistance will benefit from our time together. But as I do every morning when I turn on the shower, I'm betting God does exist, the client will benefit, and warm water will flow.

March 2016

CHAPTER 21

MY BEDEVILED SELF

Patches of green can still be found emerging through the fallen leaves covering the forest floor only yards from my Vermont home. From my office window I watch a resting crow perched on a nearby tree limb. Snow will soon blanket all I can see. The natural world appears to be peaceful and the crow's reverie comforting, but where there is quiet, a predator lurks, and where silence prevails, its prey remains cautious and alert.

A moment earlier, I was contemplating the horrific series of recent shootings, beginning with the ones in Paris in mid-November, then the ones directed at the Planned Parenthood Center in Colorado Springs, followed by the shooting rampage in San Bernardino. All of them happened in the span of about three weeks. I don't know about you, but I have difficulty processing the grief which comes from such events.

At times, my sadness and mourning for innocent victims is disturbed by my own violent eye-for-an-eye fantasies of vengeance, the unbeckoned ones that seep into my mind even as I grieve. And when they don't pass slowly through the veil between my conscious and unconscious worlds, they explode upon me without warning—in dreams, while reading, exercising, enjoying another's company, sipping a beer, or gazing into the flames of a fire.

I awaken at three o'clock, sit up and experience a brief moment of dream-induced vertigo, or at other times I blink, look away from the cozy fire, breathe deeply and resume the conversation I'm part of, and then take another sip of beer. The vertigo passes, but the images of the slain and injured do not, nor do the violent dreams tearing me out of my sleep. Thanksgiving weekend has passed, and as thankful and filled with gratitude as I am, a part of me harbors ill will toward those who commit heinous crimes.

If, as Freud believed, eliminating self-deception (not to be confused with self-examination) will give meaning to life, then I must venture into that dark place in my soul, the abyss in which I become the enemy, capable of horrific acts. However, often enough I find deception appealing and denial a sought-after state. But, good and evil, they are my thoughts, connected to my soul, and I must own them.

When current events, tragic ones in particular, provide access to those aspects of my inner world I would prefer to avoid, I must find the courage to cross the threshold into the darkness. For me to be fully human necessitates that journey, regardless of how disturbing and unsettling it is. As Barry Stevens remarked (though most often attributed to President James A. Garfield), "The truth shall set you free, but first it will make you miserable."[1]

Jesus, we're told, turned the other cheek, and asked his followers to love their enemies. Gandhi and King preached nonviolence and the pursuit of truth as the means to liberate the disenfranchised. Though their struggles differed vastly from mine, I suspect their internal journey was similar, acknowledging the demons yet keeping them at bay while living fully into what it means to be human—two aspects of my own humanness for which I express gratitude and thanks. I admire them for keeping their inner impulses (and I assume they had them) in check. Against great injustice, the desire to lash out is very tempting, and yet these three great men were able to manage not only their own frustrations but keep others from lashing out as well.

I am relaxed as I look out my office window into the peaceful forest where preparations for winter are underway. Violence and calm, savagery and order coexist in our world just as they do in the forest beyond my window. It is my hope, however, the recent violence which has marred my sleep and waking states will be resolved through peaceful methods rather than further violence. Wishful thinking perhaps, but faith in humankind's goodness keeps that hope alive.

December 2015

CHAPTER 22

GOD, IF YOU'RE LISTENING, IT'S A REASONABLE REQUEST

He wanted to die.

The woman who had been his wife, mother of his children, and best friend had preceded him in death, and he wished to join her.

What was left?

I met the parents of my best friend when I was a college student. He and his wife thought of me as one of their own, and though our contact over the years suffered long gaps, I knew my best friend's parents meant and lived by what they said—I was family.

He'd served in WWII, married his sweetheart, raised a fine family, and was an exceptional employee. He was an active member in his faith community, a team player not averse to grunt work, and by all accounts—not his own, of course—an active steward of the gifts and talents God had given him.

He is, in my opinion, God's kind of guy.

I saw him recently at his wife's memorial service. He was not ill, but infirmed by the decrements of age. The smile, affable manner, strong handshake, and upbeat approach remained intact, though a series of minor strokes had affected his speech—something he readily acknowledged by shrugging his shoulders. His passion for engagement continued to compel, just as it had been when I first met him.

At the memorial service, the reception, and later in his retirement center home, he frequently pointed to the ceiling and said "soon," a gesture directed toward a place beyond our finite knowing. Those of us who know and love him knew what he meant.

My mother, beloved and difficult in equal measure, longed to join my father who had predeceased her by twenty-six years at the time of her death in 2013. She spoke eloquently of what she anticipated heaven to be—a place of majesty where she and loved ones would gather at Jesus's feet, sing in a choir of angels, and be free from worry and pain. She never pointed toward the sky but spoke the words of hope and yearning. She, however, clung to this earthbound world, a life of worry and anxiety, with the same tenacity she'd exercised when demanding our dinner plates be clean before enjoying dessert.

I often asked her, "Why is it so difficult for you to find peace and comfort in your faith?"

"I do," she'd reply. "My faith gives me peace."

It didn't appear so to me. Nevertheless, her hope in the hereafter remained undiminished throughout her ninety-nine years, as did her incessant worrying.

When she peacefully gave in to the passing from this life into the next, I was relieved her faith had been rewarded—at least I hope so—and a lifetime of niggling worry, anxiety, and chronic second-guessing would no longer be her companions.

I sensed my close friend's father wasn't about to cling, and though he could be frustratingly stubborn I think that same trait will keep him asking his Maker, "Soon?"—and do so with a smile.

My faith is fragile, and if I point heavenward without acknowledging my doubt, I am doing the Creator and myself a disservice—my justification for keeping my restless hands in my pockets. I rail too frequently against God's silence when it is my ears which are closed to the Spirit. Too often I succumb to embracing God's absence rather than searching for his presence.

I take great pleasure in the knowledge that kind and loving people of faith experience certainty in their spiritual beliefs, and wish the same for myself.

I hope my elderly friend's raised hand is acknowledged, and the request for "soon" is granted. It seems only right for a compassionate God to do so.

And now, as for my reluctance and doubt ...

March 2015

—PART 5—

PRAYERS, PLEAS, AND CONVERSATIONS

CHAPTER 23

WHOEVER IS PRAYING FOR SNOW, PLEASE STOP

Those words could have been uttered by any number of town and city mayors, snowplow operators, or others impacted by the heavy snowfall this year, and if they were, they'd be in agreement with the message board outside the rural New England church where I noticed them.

My mother, Doris, often warned, "Be careful what you pray for," and on one occasion, when I admonished her to never end a sentence with a preposition, she responded by saying, "That's what it's about." I'm not sure what she meant, but as a sixth grader at the time, I knew I'd been scolded for taking both spiritual and secular authority lightly.

Over the years, I've become increasingly appreciative of the soothing practice of prayer, an often times random exercise, a leap of faith without attachment to the consequence or end goal. My prayerful meanderings may run the gamut from lament to gratitude, but in either case, or all scenarios in between, I don't necessarily need the snow to stop falling.

Freud believed the introspective process of psychoanalysis—throwing light on the darkest recesses of our soul—would elucidate conflict and enable us to experience the uniqueness in each of our lives. It is the process of delving into the soul and embracing the struggle between, say, depression and joy which provides to us our lives' deepest meaning.

William James, the nineteenth-century philosopher, psychologist, and physician spoke of the mind's "booming, buzzing confusion." Among his most meaningful and real-life experiences were ones in which he fleetingly experienced the presence of God, moments he often attributed to "phantasies of the brain" and frequently questioned, but nonetheless experienced with "exultation and insight."[1]

Doris Marum never published a book or lectured in front of anyone but her husband and two sons, had no degree beyond her high school diploma, but she knew some things—even when the truth and substance of what she said eluded her in practice. The sayings she declared were often met with my glazed-over gaze, and though I nodded assent, I just wanted out of there. Acknowledging her advice was the quickest ticket to wherever I was headed.

I remember rolling my eyes when she would state, "Pray as if it all depends on God, and work as if it all depends on you." Perhaps there were times when I prayed with a fervor she would have admired, and maybe I worked hard enough on occasion to warrant her approving smile, and perhaps God's. Most of the time I experienced her declarations as hectoring—pontifications to get me to do something I was reluctant to do or not do at all.

Though I've often been reluctant to buy into their ideas completely, Sigmund Freud and William James have provided much of the underpinning for my view of our inner world of the soul, and how we struggle with emotional conflict to live the best life possible. My mother, bless her heart, spoke words of truth, and even though I questioned her embodiment of them—she was frequently spot-on (another preposition).

It is still snowing in Boston, so I'm not sure whose prayers, if any, are being heard.

February 2015

CHAPTER 24

BOB DYLAN AND THE CUBS

Game Four of the 2016 World Series played last night in Chicago and was won by the Cleveland Indians, who now lead the best-of-seven series three games to one. Timely hitting and good-at-bats (taking pitches, getting walks or a base on balls) continue to elude the Cubs. To be fair, the club from Cleveland has played quite well.

While the link between the Cubs and Dylan may seem far-fetched at best, for a moment, please indulge me.

This year's Nobel Laureate in Literature, Bob Dylan, has remained quintessentially Dylan-like by not responding in public to the announcement he was awarded the 2016 Nobel Prize for Literature. But that said, he's not granted an interview in two years—unusual in this age of social media when everybody has something to say about everything, but not, however, unusual for Dylan. Fortunately, Ben Sisario spoke with the troubadour and wrote about the interview in *Bob Dylan Speaks, At Last, on His Nobel*.

Here's the connection: My fan-of-his-music relationship with Bob Dylan goes back as far as my attachment to the Cubs—college days. Just as the Cubs are my favorite sports team, Bob Dylan and his backup group, The Band, are my favorite rock 'n rollers. Martin Scorsese's 1978 film, *The Last Waltz,* The Band's last concert, remains among my favorite paeans to rock 'n roll—a notch above *Woodstock.*

Dylan's award announcement and the Cubs' playoff run came together for me when I read a Dylan quote in the Sisario article: "You have to write a hundred bad songs before you write one good one."[1] I thought the World Series banner's sentiment, "One hundred and eight years to get a winner," takes patience. So does working the lyrics and composition of one hundred songs before hitting on the right one. This doesn't mean the efforts in between were for naught—some good tunes were written and great baseball seasons played, just not the "big prize" result each attempt was designed to create. I'm pleased Dylan has been acknowledged for his words and music, and I hope the Cubs can persevere this week and in so doing capture the big prize they've been waiting so long for and working hard to win.

I attended Sunday morning worship service today, a commitment I made back in January of this year when I decided to be a regular attendee, a new direction in my spiritual odyssey. The purpose has been to find answers to my lifelong questions about the relevance and existence of God. This day God had little chance, as my thoughts were consumed by music and baseball. Like Dylan and the Cubs, my struggles at solving my soul's puzzles seem futile— answers like the big prize or knock-it-out-of-the-park lyrics elude me. I discard fruitless attempts, strike out many times, but then there are times like this morning that keep me coming back.

A parishioner, sitting within my line of vision, a man who, like me, attends a monthly men's breakfast at the church, appeared distracted and teary-eyed, lost in his own hurt. After he walked by my pew to exit the sanctuary, I waited a few moments, then decided to seek him out.

When we met in the hallway, I asked him how he was doing. He said he wanted a cup of coffee, and his wife, who'd been in remission from cancer, had learned the day before the cancer had returned and was metastatic. I listened, then offered to keep his family's struggles in my conversations with God, and assured him he could email or call me anytime. Before we left the church, he to check on his young daughters and I to go for a bike ride, he wiped the tears from his cheeks, smiled, and said, "Go Cubs!"

My thoughts implored the God whose existence I question to act, while my own watery eyes forced me to pull into a quiet spot near the local market where I said, "Thank you."

October 2016

CHAPTER 25

THOUGHTS AND PRAYERS

"My thoughts and prayers are with you and your family in this time of loss," is what I said.

Moments later, if not while uttering those words, their well-intentioned but hollow and generic nature seeped into my consciousness.

Mark Leibovich, in a *New York Times Magazine* article, titled "So Sorry," addresses the platitudinous use of the phrase *thoughts and prayers.* I'd questioned the use of that particular phrase and others like it before discovering his well-researched and written essay, which helped me revisit my own reliance on euphemisms—toned-down words or phrases which are substituted for blunt, more direct ones, like *passed* or *time of loss* when I meant *died.*

Finding words accurately conveying feelings of sympathy and condolence can be difficult, but here's a sentence more consistent with my sentiment than the opening line of this post: "I am thinking about you and your family and offering prayers of healing and comfort for all of you as you mourn your father's death." The first sentence is generic and lacks the intimacy and active engagement of the second one.

Too often, I fall back on clichés to soften hard moments of suffering and anguish. Listening to my own and others' feelings is important, and if lessening the brutality of a harsh reality is warranted, so be it. (For example, is there any reason to say, "I'm terribly sorry your daughter was killed in the car crash"?) The focus, in any case, should be on their suffering and helping to lessen it than to recall the reason for it, unless they wish to recount events, which can also have a healing effect. Likewise, being protected in times of adversity makes sense, and using expressions in line with that sensibility demonstrate kindness, caring, and love.

I enjoy words and their usage. Reading, writing, and speaking, employing the linguistic forms as vehicles, bring me in touch with the feelings and thoughts they communicate. That said, I also know when I use them flippantly or with a callousness which is mindless and perfunctory, lacking genuine affect.

"I feel your pain" may have been a 90's phrase offering consolation (Mark Leibovich attributes its popularity to Bill Clinton), but it seems to be a hackneyed if not trivializing statement of identification with the listener's lament or despair. I recall an occasion when I spoke those words to a friend who was suffering. As I offered them my lips parted in a not-too-disguised wrinkle of a smile. My friend responded to the facial expression rather than my thought. "Why are you smiling?" he asked.

"Because as I was speaking, I realized the emptiness of my words," I replied. And then I responded to him with words reflecting the sentiment I felt for him—love, and a recognition of the awfulness he was experiencing.

A phrase which has defined a Winter Term course I've taught at Middlebury College—"our electronic devices make the distant close, but the close distant"—applies equally well to shallow expressions of feeling. Their expression implies a closeness, perhaps a kinship of feeling, but in truth creates distance by their reflexive and generic use.

Words are powerful tools, and the feelings that evoke them can be compelling. When we react in horror, disbelief, and intense anguish to an event—mass killings, the death of a loved one, a terrorist attack—finding words to adequately describe the feelings and our connection(s) to what created them can be difficult.

Recently I attended a showing of the film *The Martian*, and during the final scenes, director Ridley Scott depicted a global outpouring of joyous sentiment which appeared to me, as a viewer, to be the authentic expression of feelings— the opposite of the anxiety and fear the film had stirred in me moments before.

As I left the theater, the stirrings of those emotions brought to mind Mark Leibovich's essay, and my own temptations to use words which distance and protect me from my own feelings as well as those of others.

I can't feel others' pain, but I do feel empathy for them. I do think about and actively pray for those I know, as well as many I read about who suffer. I think and feel my way and sometimes struggle to use words conveying my honest thoughts and feelings, and when I catch myself in the hollowness of generic expressions, I try to dig deeper.

November 2015

CHAPTER 26

NOISE ABATEMENT

The gift, a harmony of silence and solitude, arrived while I was preoccupied by the endless chatter of my annoying self—a musing to which no respectable psychotherapist, let alone a well-analyzed one, should submit.

The surreal "present" occurred around six o'clock, January 25, 2018, sometime after I'd settled into the welcome anonymity of the back seat of my friend's SUV, stretched the seat belt strap across my body and inserted the tongue into the buckle by my right hip.

I was buckled up, but not for the ride I was about to take.

David, his wife Marsha, and I (and Siri too if virtual assistants count) had begun the hour-long drive to Norwood, Massachusetts, for a dinner party with college classmates. The following day, Friday, we would gather again at a celebrative memorial for Don, our deceased classmate. While my two friends in the front seat drifted in and out of conversation, I watched as the darkened world outside my window passed by. The long stretches of unremarkable steel and concrete noise abatement walls captured my attention. These structures had no relevance to me, but on this particular evening I became intrigued, if not compelled, by their presence along the highway.

Their poignant place in my inner journey would soon be apparent.

Thoughts of Don and his family, friendship, the brevity of life—even a fully lived one—vied for my attention with incessant negative self-talk, a pattern which often happens when school reunions occur, a time when I'm painfully reminded of how lonely I felt during my high school and college years—feelings I tried to hide. *You're not good enough, and you never fulfilled your potential. You don't measure up to your college classmates. You're a divorced reluctant disciple among successfully married, doubt-free "disciples."*

I'd recently read a poem, *Church Porch*, by George Herbert and recalled part of the verse:

> By all means use sometimes to be alone;
> Salute thyself, see what thy soul doth wear;
> Dare to look in thy chest, for 'tis thine own,
> And tumble up and down what thou find'st there—[1]

Tumble mode found me in the darkness of the backseat.

The litany of mistakes, miscues, and failures seemed endless. I fought to give memories of Don more than a toehold as we crossed the state line from New Hampshire to Massachusetts. I pictured his smile, heard his laughter, recalled his wonderful wry sense of humor, and remembered with fondness our shared wonderings about whether we fit or were misfits during our college days.

And then my preoccupation with the noise abatement walls began to make sense. Frederick Buechner came to mind, a wise and insightful writer whose words often bring me hope and solace. I knew the gist of what he'd written, and that was enough at the time as I gazed out the window, but days later I looked up the quote in his work, *Telling the Truth:* "Beneath our clothes, our reputations, our pretensions, beneath our religion or lack of it, we are all vulnerable both to the storm without and to the storm within, and if ever we are to find true shelter, it is with the recognition of our tragic nakedness and need for true shelter that we have to start."[2]

I needed an inner earthen berm, an impervious masonry noise abatement wall to stop the ceaseless chatter. The poet and writer were taking me there, and so too was Paul Tillich. The Winter Term course I'd been teaching was coming up on the final week of class, and I'd referenced Tillich's distinction between loneliness and solitude as students immersed themselves in questions about the loneliness of their virtual lives on social media platforms. "Language has created the word 'loneliness' to express the pain of being alone," he'd written, "and it has created the word 'solitude' to express the glory of being alone."[3]

As I relived the loneliness of bygone college days, my painful feelings of inadequacy began to ebb as Don's humor, his smile and genuineness found more than a tenuous grip in my soul. Silence and solitude, an embraceable companionship, brought a needed smidgen of glory to being alone with myself at that moment, and to myself as I've always been.

City streets replaced the Interstate. Storefronts and residential homes passed by outside where the protective noise pollution walls had defined the landscape. Noise abatement, the kind troubled souls seek in despairing times of self-doubt, had quelled my raucous internal prattle at least for the moment, and provided desired respite.

Do we not all struggle and wrestle with unnecessary, yet very real, doubts and questions about our worthiness, value, roles and place? Of course, we do, this reluctant disciple and psychotherapist included.

During an imagined meeting, one where I intruded on Jesus and Freud, I pulled up a chair, set my glass of beer on the table, interrupted their conversation and asked: "Are doubt and darkness necessary to see the light?"

They hesitated, as if each was waiting for the other to respond, then set their own beers on the table and smiled.

They've taught me well.

February 2018

CHAPTER 27

CHRISTMAS AND BEYOND

You're a private soul, perhaps a stoic New Englander. I don't know you well enough to say, and it doesn't matter. Either or both may apply and explain your reluctance to go public with your recently diagnosed illness—public, that is, beyond close family, old friends, and your church community.

I respect and understand that.

A mutual acquaintance told me you have been sick, a form of cancer, undergoing treatments, and dealing with the side effects of chemotherapy. You're a carpenter. I'm a psychologist. You were an employed worker, and I, your employer, but those labels don't capture the truth of two men who met over a job.

We share a faith, a belief in a loving God and a risen Christ, a fellowship which goes beyond work and paychecks. You became and continue to be part of my daily meditations and prayer life.

Our Christmas tree now standing decked in snow outside our glass French doors is a magnificent reminder of God's presence and the ties that bind all of us, however or whatever the circumstances bringing our paths together.

You and your family are in my prayers.

Roger

January 2019

CHAPTER 28

MY NEW FRIEND

The email you wrote in January was encouraging and hopeful. You thanked me for thinking of you and your family ("Christmas and Beyond") and expressed hope you would soon be healthy and back to a normal routine. A week or two later, you wrote again and mentioned driving past Highland Way, wanting to stop in to say hi, but didn't because you needed to get to your daughter's house. "Next time I'll call," you wrote, "bring lunch or we can meet somewhere to talk, share more of our stories, faith journeys, and over a meal we'll get to know each other better."

In my reply I wrote, "I'm looking forward to that. Continue to get well."

Now I've been told you died this morning.

My sadness pales in comparison to that of your grieving family, beloved friends, and members of your church community. They already knew the person I looked forward to getting to know. Nonetheless you touched my life, a kindred soul and fellow sojourner; a man who shared his faith in a brave and thoughtful manner. With you there was no preaching or instructing. You didn't need to say what was evident, just the simple truth: *this is who I am.*

In our last conversation I mentioned, with some discomfort and embarrassment, I often wrestle and struggle in my faith. "Me too," you replied, "but I know God loves me."

Thank you, Ken. Your family and friends are in my prayers.

Roger

February 2019

CHAPTER 29

TALKING TO MYSELF WHILE RECITING HER WORDS

Eleanor Roosevelt had a habit of writing on her hands, the very hands that had clasped those of haves and have-nots by the thousands, kings, queens, and common folk alike, my mother's included when they exchanged greetings at a small-town gathering. Perhaps the seed thoughts and personal, nuanced words for this prayer were etched or scrawled between the lifelines on those same palms. Whether they were or not, and I like to believe snippets were, Eleanor Roosevelt's favorite prayer touches my soul's yearnings, and so I share her words with you.

> Our Father, who has set a restlessness in our hearts and made us all seekers after that which we can never fully find, forbid us to be satisfied with what we make of life. Draw us from base content and set our eyes on far-off goals. Keep us at tasks too hard for us that we may be driven to Thee for strength. Deliver us from fretfulness and self-pitying; make us sure of the good we cannot see and of the hidden good in the world. Open our eyes to simple beauty all around us and our hearts to the loveliness men hide from us because we do not try to understand them. Save us from ourselves and show us a vision of the world made new.[1]

The hope-filled message of Advent transcends any season or embraced beliefs. My head kept a ceaseless, rhythmic nodding as I read these sentences and whispered, *Thank you, Eleanor,* and *yes, me too,* and then I smiled as I finished her final prayerful request.

December 2017

—PART 6—

GRATEFUL OR ALL THINGS PERFECT AND FLAWED, INCLUDING LOVE

CHAPTER 30

WAKING UP TO GRATITUDE, AND BEING GRATEFUL
SLEEP IS OVER, AT LEAST FOR NOW

Ollie, the beloved camel and resident of the Round Barn Merinos working sheep farm, died on Saturday, February 22, 2020. His presence in the pasture among indigenous sheep always brought a smile to my face as I commuted along US 7 to my Middlebury office. I wasn't alone. Travelers and tourists frequently pulled over on the roadside and posed for selfies with the irrepressible two-humped Bactrian camel—close-ups which seemed to please all the participants in the photo shoot.

I'm saddened by his death, and only now in his absence made aware of how much fun and joy Ollie's presence brought me, especially on days when commuter doldrums or weighty personal or professional issues put me in a funk. While speeding by, I often imagined him winking all or one of the four eyelids on his left or right eye, checking out curiosity seekers while maintaining a regal posture—curious and aloof in camel-like fashion.

My iconic four-legged Ferrisburgh neighbor's death awakened me. His death confronted me with a habit of taking for granted life events and people whose paths cross mine. I miss large and small pleasures when preoccupied—a frequent state of mind. Paying attention opens me to moments when loved ones and friends, patients, acquaintances, and even strangers can enrich and make a difference in my life. Life is short, too brief for the unnecessary "sleep" which seduces me into taking life for granted. I foolishly adhere to the idea of permanence when impermanence is life's constant message.

Thank you, Ollie.

Author Denis Johnson states: "Write naked. That means to write what you would never say. Write in blood. As if ink is so precious you can't waste it. Write in exile, as if you are never going to get home again, and you have to call back every detail."[1]

Though his words are intended for writers, they may also apply to my practice of gratitude. May I be thankful with naked abandon, grateful in life-giving word and deed, express gratitude in ways I've thought but shunned—too embarrassed, proud, or posturing to preserve a self-image, but doing so now as if it's my only opportunity to do so.

During David Marchese's interview with Sonny Rollins in *The New York Times Magazine,* the saxophone colossus reflects on a lifetime of being grateful "that he was able to do music," and "that giving is better than getting."[2]

Loved ones and family have embraced me with love for which I'm grateful, especially during those times when I've been testy and difficult, a distant partner.

Friends have likewise been loving, even in times when they've rolled their eyes at "Roger being Roger," but nonetheless stayed faithful in their love. I'm grateful for them.

It has been a privilege, which I embrace with gratitude, to be engaged in the practice of the gentle art of psychotherapy, to be invited into people's lives to share in their sorrows and joy. Thank you for inviting me in.

In the opening scene of Shakespeare's play, *The Second Part of King Henry the Sixth,* Henry states: "Oh , that lends me life, lend me a heart replete with thankfulness!"[3] My version, expressed daily but too often by rote goes like this: "Jesus Christ, have mercy on me, and for your gifts, named and unnamed, known and unknown, remembered and forgotten, I give you thanks." I often add, like the man who dropped to his knees at Jesus's feet, "I believe; help my unbelief."

If I've tested the love of others by harmful words and flawed behavior I've certainly done the same with God, whose existence and commitment I challenge, question, and frequently doubt. I'm grateful for God's unwavering love, and though not always showing it in my life, I am brought to my knees in gratitude.

One week has passed since Ollie died. This morning, as I drove into nearby Vergennes with trash and materials for recycling, I slowed to a crawl going by the pasture where he'd grazed and roamed. Traffic was light, and I saw no cars following me. I carefully placed a wreath next to the lone bouquet of flowers attached to the post and wire fence which kept the animals safe. The pasture was empty, but I smiled and waved anyway, grateful for memories and my reawakening to gratitude. Ollie's death occurred as I'd thought about gratitude (and that's the rub, *thinking* about it rather than *being* grateful), reminding me to be actively open to mystery, to resist the ease of taking life for granted, and stop putting off until tomorrow what stirs in my soul today.

March 2020

CHAPTER 31

SO WHAT?—GRACE AND ACCEPTANCE

Several days ago, I listened to *Kind of Blue,* all six tracks of the innovative recording by Miles Davis, but I played the opening track, "So What," over and over. I never tire of listening to his creative and inventive music, an indispensable part of my jazz library, and on this occasion while repeating the first track, I imagined a meeting between Jesus and Miles. An event which, if it occurred (and I hope a facsimile of my imaginings did happen), it was with an outpouring of grace—God's unmerited favor.

Jimmy Cobb, the drummer in the Miles Davis Quintet at the time of the studio recording, even remarked with reverence: "[*Kind of Blue*] must have been made in heaven."[1]

Maybe so, and though I know it is a studio album recorded at Columbia in New York City, something of the divine threads its way through the tones and melodies of the recording which belies its humble, earthbound creation on 30th Street.

As I listened, the tunes spurred images of a forgiving God of grace and his loving Son, Jesus, standing with a brooding Miles Davis, musical genius and trumpeter, who might question or be overwhelmed by Jesus's unmerited favor and embrace in a heavenly setting of unconditional acceptance. But that's grace.

I could see Jesus, the Prince of Peace, carpenter, and Son of God, with outstretched arms greet Miles Davis, the Prince of Darkness, upon the latter's arrival in heaven. The famous musician was given the nickname because of his aloof, brooding, and at times combative personality.

"Play something for me, please," says the Prince of Peace.

Miles looks over the rim of his sunglasses but maintains his taciturn stance.

"I beg you?" requests the Galilean, who has also known great suffering.

Intrigued by his entreaty, the trumpeter turns away from his host and begins to play.

Jesus stands in awe, and when the last note fades into silence he bows. "Welcome, my son," he says. "That was beautiful!"

Miles slowly turns to face his gracious host and without removing his sunglasses, he declares, "Thank *you*."

Jesus, the embodiment of openness, unconditional acceptance, and limitless empathy, draws the musician into his embrace. "I know it well," he replies. "The first track, 'So What,' on your album. Gabriel plays it often."

Theologian Frederick Buechner believes the Jesus story and the gift of grace (unconditional acceptance) introduce us to the possibility of wholeness (shelter from the storm): "Beneath our clothes, our reputations, our pretensions, beneath our religion or lack of it, we are all vulnerable both to the storm without and the storm within, and if ever we are to find shelter, it is with the recognition of our tragic nakedness and need for true shelter that we have to start."[2]

I often look in the mirror and, to my chagrin, see pretention and brokenness.

Miles Davis experienced the "dark night of the soul" in ways foreign to me. He was subjected to racist taunts and behaviors, and he struggled with addictive behaviors. He and I do share what Buechner describes as being "…

vulnerable to the storm without and the storm within ... and the recognition of our tragic nakedness ..."[3]

Miles Davis, despite being chained to addiction, heard the divine in his soul. The inestimable value of each of us, the gift each of us is meant to be, is made possible through the bounty of divine grace.

June 2017

CHAPTER 32

WORDS ARE IMPORTANT

My appreciation for the importance of words increases with every op-ed column, news report, and magazine article I read. Perhaps it is a sign of the times. I've always had great respect for the words of authors whose books I lose myself in, and I have discovered anew their importance and value as I write these short pieces for the website. Three authors, one with whom I've shared inspiring conversations and the other two whose written words give me hope, recently reentered my Advent life through their comforting words.

A California friend, Bill Doulos, sent me a copy of the homily he delivered at The Church of Our Saviour on November 27, the title of which is "Join In Our Crusade!," an invitation "to be an evangelistic outreach and a beacon of compassion for our neighbors in the San Gabriel Valley and beyond."[1]

Bill founded Jubilee Homes, a network of homes whose residents are in recovery and transition from substance abuse and incarceration. Bill and his supporters provide a safe and healthy living space for the healing of soul, mind, and body before residents reenter the world. His quotation from Victor Hugo's *Les Miserables* grabbed my soul, but more on that in a moment.

Henri Nouwen in *Bread for the Journey: A Daybook of Wisdom and Faith* provides daily encouragement with words which bolster my faith. His brief thoughts on the December 10 entry, titled *The Peaceable Kingdom,* restored my faltering Advent soul: "All of creation belongs together in the arms of its Creator. The final vision is that not only will all men and women recognize that they are brothers and sisters called to live in unity, but all members of God's creation will come together in complete harmony."[2]

Words are important.

Jean Valjean, whose apocalyptic vision was cited by Bill Doulos in his homily, captured my attention when he exhorts us to stand with him, be strong, and seek beyond our limited vision. If we listen we can hear the distant songs and music of others, love them, and in so doing see the face of God.

The aforementioned authors, Doulos, Hugo, and Nouwen speak of apocalyptic visions, but not in the dire terms I've become accustomed to think—imminent disaster, cataclysm, large-scale destruction, even annihilation.

I read and reread their words, searching for personal terminology which would carry me beyond the doom and gloom words and phrases to those more closely aligned with my seasonal thoughts and feelings. In my pursuit, I scoured a variety of definitions for apocalyptic, and settled on the one coinciding with my segueing into Advent—an event of "momentous consequence."

Words are important.

Victor Hugo's character, Jean Valjean, renews my faith as he calls for imagining a time of song when a distant drum calls me to stand strong, see beyond the barricade, and to live more fully into the better part of my self.

Henri Nouwen lovingly, but with the firmness of spare words admonishes me: "We must keep this vision alive."

Bill Doulos asks in the closing words of his homily, "Will you join in our crusade?"

Yes, is my response, *I will.*

December 2016

CHAPTER 33

DID YOU HAVE A GOOD FLIGHT?

"... love Dad, and journeying mercies be with you throughout your travels."

These words, regardless of whether a physical journey was being planned or in progress, were also the closing, parting words in many of my father's letters, his face-to-face "goodbyes." They often referred to my "travels" as a boy developing into a young man, and then into a spiritually conscious adult. Recalling those words of hope and grace while returning home to Vermont from a recent California trip brought a needed smile to my face, and a respite of patience and peace to my soul. Here's the backstory.

It was a short flight from San Francisco to Long Beach, California, and as usual I'd prepared well for it. *The New York Times* was open to the sports page, *Real Jazz* was playing a song by Trombone Shorty on the in-flight audio, and I was enjoying the natural light from my window seat in 9F. Passengers were patient but focused, lined up in the aisle looking for their seats and spots to store carry-on bags, none more so than the stern-faced woman who ushered a smiling little girl in a white pinafore (her granddaughter I assumed) into seat 9E.

"Sit still until I finish," she said, pointing her index finger at the well-behaved child. I watched the woman's practiced moves as she swabbed all the surfaces the little girl might touch with several Clorox Handi-Wipes. I admired her efficiency and thoroughness as much as I did her charge's obedience as she cleaned. When she appeared to be almost done, I interrupted her mission to ask if she'd like me to wipe the armrest the little girl and I would share.

"That's quite all right," she replied, "but thank you for asking."

When she was safely buckled in, the little girl's feet, in white Mary Jane shoes to match her dress, barely extended over the edge of her seat. She and I exchanged smiles and she declared, "I'm excited because we're going to Disneyland. Are you too?"

"No," I replied, "but I'm excited because I'm going to see friends."

The elder woman placed a sandwich on the tray table which captured my seatmate's undivided attention. I resumed reading *The New York Times* and listening to music. Following a smooth flight and a quick taxi to the gate, my two fellow travelers prepared to disembark, but before doing so the precocious little girl asked me if I'd had a good flight.

"Yes," I said, "and you?"

"Me too," she replied politely. Her grandmother smiled as they exited the row and walked down the aisle.

Work and pleasure, time with clients and friends, mixed well during the ensuing busy week in the Los Angeles area, and though I enjoy visits to my California roots, returning to my home in Vermont is something I cherish. I savored these newly formed memories as I boarded my flight for the return trip from LAX to JFK. A creature of some habit, I'd booked seat 9F for this leg of the trip as well. I found my seat, turned on *Real Jazz*, and settled in for the flight.

Though looking forward to returning to the state I now call home, there was a restlessness in my heart about leaving loved ones and clients after this short visit. Illness and aging, troubling life circumstances among friends, family members, and clients occupied my thoughts. When I opened the *LA Times,* so too did the disturbing headlines of a world in flux and chaos, frequently shaped by thoughtless posturing self-serving leaders.

A young overweight man seated himself in the middle seat next to me. We shared a nodded greeting as he began to situate himself. While struggling with the seat belt his right elbow came in contact with my audio controls on the armrest between our seats. This motion instantly changed my audio channels from soft straight-ahead jazz to raucous, full-volume grunge. I tapped on his arm, pointed to the controls and he lip synced an apology. This sequence occurred several more times once we reached our cruising altitude, and each time he was apologetic. The audio intrusions stopped after I established my left elbow as an immovable barrier between us.

Pleased about the pilot's announcement that a strong tail wind would bring us into JFK an hour ahead of schedule, I turned on the flight map to find our location. As I was viewing the route over Iowa my seatmate edged forward in his seat and then bent over his laptop. With a dexterity that comes with practice he unabashedly began sticking the pinky and index fingers of both hands into his right and left nostrils respectively—left-hand fingers plumbed the left and right-hand fingers the right. When all four digits were topped with whatever he'd been mining for, he didn't reach for a hanky or tissue but instead wiped his fingers clean on the back of the passenger seat in front of him. This occurred on three or four separate occasions, but it wasn't until he began eating airline snacks with those same fingers that the magnitude of my disgust made me bristle.

Thoughts of the engaging little girl from flight 424 and her cleanliness-conscious grandmother swirled in my mind but brought little relief from my abhorrent and nauseating present reality. I closed my eyes, but a mindful practice eluded me. A ballad by Miles Davis couldn't make a dent in my loathing of the man next to me. The offense to my sensibilities filled my soul. Looking out the window brought perspective because the view of the plains over thirty-five thousand feet below made me aware of how small I am, and how insignificant my abhorrence, wounded sensibilities, loathing and disgust in a less myopic world view. Are we not all flawed and equal? Why had I not offered him a tissue?

"Mercy is radical kindness. Mercy means offering or being offered aid in desperate straits. Mercy is not deserved. It involves absolving the un-absolvable, forgiving the unforgivable," writes Anne Lamott.[1] Her words brought me comfort as I absolved myself of righteousness, and my fellow passenger of his uncouthness. Finding ways to be humble, embrace humility, and be confident in that arduous process, accept otherness and in so doing avoid the trap of self-righteous thinking, trips me up over and over and over again.

I do want to practice loving and forgiveness, but too often only when it's easy, not humbling. And when it stretches me, is difficult, challenging, and tests my self-centered perception of how things ought to be, I resist. Lesson learned, for now at least.

Whenever I think I've "got it," God and the universe are bound to seat me next to a nose-picker to remind me of my own feet of clay, and how much of a work in progress I continue to be.

Traveling mercies, Dad, and thanks.

April 2018

CHAPTER 34

PASSIONATE

Finding people and events which bring a smile and uplift my soul requires being open to the incidental and unexpected.

The arborist, editor, and tire man did just that. Their presence in my life is not a miracle, I don't think, though I could be mistaken, but are they incidental gifts, unexpected epiphanies?

Absolutely.

They're the kind of presents we too frequently overlook, or worse yet, dismiss. At least I do.

Not this time. And as the holiday season unfolds, I'm grateful my busyness and myopic preoccupation with self gets derailed by the gift of their presence, a gift which brings me pleasure, needed hope, and joy.

A timely invitation to Thanksgiving and Advent.

It began on a November morning, Monday the thirteenth to be exact. I'd opened my laptop, and while the screen came to life I took delight in the sun's rays streaming through the forest beyond my home-office window. The day ahead included typical activities: writing, reading, responding to emails, exercise, and several appointments in my home office. The atypical events included the arrival of Gregory, an arborist, to cut down and remove several wind-damaged trees, a detailed reading and response to an email from Roy (dismissively scanned the night before)—an editor and friend—as well as an appointment with Wayne to have all-weather tires mounted on my Volvo.

My second cup of coffee, still steaming, was in its place on the desk to my right when I was startled by the unmistakable revving-up growl of a chainsaw. I put on a hoodie and walked out to greet Gregory and his two assistants. They politely refused my offer of coffee, and after a brief conversation they began their work, Gregory deftly measuring and sawing while the two others hauled cuttings to a wood-chipper and tossed larger pieces into their truck. Gregory, whom I'd met eleven years ago, has always been efficient and thorough in the jobs he's done for me, but what I saw on this morning was the joy he puts into and receives from his craft.

He specializes in the care, love, and maintenance of all species of trees. He employs a chainsaw with the dexterity, grace, and precision with which a sushi chef uses knives—an extension of his deceptively strong arms. In his hands, a stump-cutter glides across the surface the way a Miele vacuum cleaner does on a fine carpet. He respectfully walks among saplings, shrubbery, old and new growth, displaying a reverence for all.

I recalled an incident involving him that occurred several years ago. A neighbor, in my presence, once referred to a tree in our yard as a "worthless weed." Gregory wistfully looked into the branches, touched the trunk of the fifteen-foot perennial plant and politely but firmly replied, "It is a *Juniperus virginiana*, a healthy Eastern cedar. It will outlive us."

I returned to my computer and opened Roy's email which included an attachment, titled *RMC Book Collection Notes*, a draft of the chapter he's contributing to an "edited volume of the history of Christian publishing." He's been an editor for over four decades and a book collector for most of that time as well.

Roy and I have known each other for almost twenty years. Though we live on opposite coasts and rarely see each other, we stay in touch online. His love of books may only be rivaled by his love of running, something I once shared with him, but now vicariously enjoy through his journal entries. I downloaded and read the attachment listing some of his collection. Melville, Davies, Kidd, Kierkegaard, MacDonald, Brooks, Murakami, and Sendak are among the authors whose collected works he owns and treasures. The 214 books on the history of book publishing and writing in the US for the nineteenth, twentieth, and twenty-first centuries is his most important collection. He has also collected a copy of every translation of the Bible in English published in the last seventy-five years in the US, including a rare copy of the Lamsa Bible, and a leather-bound Scofield Bible autographed by the scholars on the translating committee.

I reread Roy's list of collected works twice, marveled at the variety of authors on the list, and then unexpectedly began a third reading, but this time focusing on the between-the-lines love and affection he has for both the written word and the books in which they're printed. His joy was contagious, not just because we share a love for books, but because I found pleasure in his joy.

Later, I pulled up the driveway where Wayne of Wayne's Tires greeted me. The constant low whirring of the air compressor would soon give way to the pneumatic impact wrench he skillfully employed to remove and then later re-secure the lug nuts on the Volvo's four tire rims. Wayne has been taking care of my car's tire needs for ten years. He replaces the regular tires with "snows" as winter approaches and takes them off when winter turns to spring. We chat a bit about business and the weather, occasionally about local politics, and about tires, a subject he knows well, and not just because it's his vocation—he loves working with them.

This day, primed by my earlier conversation with Gregory and response to Roy's email, I asked him, "Why tires?" and how long he'd been working with them. He said he'd opened the shop thirty years ago and hadn't had a moment's regret. He mentioned the importance of being his own boss and employee, an independent work life which suited him.

"When I do my job well," he continued, "customers like you feel safe and confident on the road, and that's important. It's a simple job," he said, "but like anything else, doing it well takes more than the simple effort of removing and replacing tires. I like people to feel good when they leave my shop, and the best way to assure that is for me to take pride in doing my job to the best of my ability. I love doing tires, and I hope it shows in my work."

"It does," I replied.

Three men in vastly different vocations, who exhibit both pride and joy in their work, is refreshing. All too often people work for money and little else. Though I've cut down trees, embraced books, and replaced tires, these gentlemen's respective love and attachment to their occupations demonstrate passion my efforts didn't. I often take for granted my own passion for the practice of psychotherapy because it's what I do. Gregory, Roy, and Wayne reconnected me with what I can easily take for granted—the joy and pleasure in committing to the work of something for which you have passion. When I keep myself open to a world which can frequently be perceived as routine, I may be visited by the incidental gift and the unexpected epiphany, for which I'm grateful.

November 2017

—PART 7—

FINDING HOPE IN PLAIN SPEAKING

CHAPTER 35

PURGATORY FALLS

Opportunities for virtuous deeds or black-hearted thinking occur regularly for me. The former I readily embrace, and the sneakiness or all-too-humanness of the latter trip me up. A perfect example of this occurred on the outskirts of Milford, New Hampshire, during a recent visit to Purgatory Falls, appropriately named for my frame of mind that day.

An early summer downpour in the morning left the trailhead's unpaved parking lot puddled and muddy. Two junky-looking cars occupied more than their fair share of parking space. The white Honda's lower side panels and wheel wells were eaten through with rust, and the dirty Ford pickup had no hub caps and a bald spare for a left rear tire.

Who would own such vehicles? White trash? Will we meet on the trail? Rushing to judgment, I notice such things and wish I didn't.

At the trailhead's entrance, I encountered a glass-encased bulletin board with trail map and hiker information, but the footlocker-sized boulder next to it captured my attention and intrigued me. On its uneven surface were two rocks. A large zucchini-shaped stone had been balanced atop a walnut-sized rock whose rough and rounded surface nonetheless kept the large stone upright and perfectly balanced.

Kids, maybe, I thought, and began the ten-minute hike to Lower Purgatory Falls.

The post-downpour scattering of showers had stopped and an eerie stillness surrounded me as I walked into the forest. Red oak and white pine trees provided a partial canopy and the low-lying cloud cover increased the ghostly atmosphere of the woods.

A palpable feeling of being watched accompanied me as I navigated over and around slippery rocks, exposed tree roots, and pooling waters.

Were the owners of the vehicles at the trailhead stalking me?

Certain the lush greenery was hiding watchful eyes, I stopped on occasion, held my breath and listened for sounds in the silence. None occurred, and I resumed my short trek. The white blazes, appropriately spaced along the path, allayed my fears. Though no one walked within earshot of me, it was clear this was a well-trodden path.

The sound of falling water distracted me from the mysterious silence of the woods, and when I reached the crest of a small knoll the falls appeared. Seated beneath where I stood were four people hunkered down between two jagged rocks: two scruffy-looking men, a scantily clad woman—all three tatted—and what appeared to be the woman's three- or four-year-old daughter. The adults were passing a homemade glass bong, and were either doing crack cocaine or smoking weed.

Trying not to stare, I made my way down the path as the little girl waved and smiled. I returned her gestures and gave an impassive head nod to the three adults. Their inscrutable nodding acknowledged if not mimicked mine.

Moving away from them, I found a rock on which to sit and take in the falls and rock formations. The intrusive judgmental thinking triggered by their presence remained vibrant, too present and unrelenting.

What lowlifes to be doing drugs with a child present. Am I safe, and what about the child? Should I say something? No, of course not, and mind your own business.

The restlessness persisted as I left my perch to hike above the falls, wanting another vantage point from which to view the falling water. I also hoped physical exertion would at least mute my unwanted thoughts, if not get rid of them. After walking around the rim of the falls I returned to sit by the darkened pool of water at its base.

The group had split up. The woman sat on a log above the water's edge, and the bearded fellow had lifted the youngster onto his shoulders, where she sat giggling and pointing at the falls. The third adult, the bald-headed younger man, had walked out to a slab of rock, a promontory jutting out above the pool about thirty feet from me, and surrounded himself with an assortment of multi-shaped-and-sized rocks he'd pulled from the water's edge. He began arranging them one on top of the other—an unimaginable balancing of size and shape which reminded me of hoodoos and fairy chimneys I'd seen in Utah and Arizona.

Mesmerized by his focus, gentle touch, and selective sculptor's eye for fitting large and small, rough and smooth stones into a pattern, I watched a sculpture take exquisite shape, a creation of beauty I suspect only he envisioned.

When he finished, or stepped back to view his work, I walked over to him and said, "Very impressive and beautiful."

He replied, "Thank you. I do this all the time. I have poor balance, an equilibrium issue preventing me from doing many normal activities. But I have an uncanny sense of balance when it comes to arranging and shaping articles provided by nature." He turned around and pointed to a tapestry of leaves and twigs behind him. "I did this before you came." The multi-tiered leaf and wood structure was stunning in design and color.

"You're very talented," I said. "Between your creations and the falls, I'm in the presence of the holy."

"You and me both," he replied, and we shook hands.

I returned to the parking lot in a state of "forest-bathing" as the woods and nature wrapped itself around me—filled with the beauty a man created, someone I'll most likely never see again, but will also never forget. No threatening creatures stalked the woods as I walked back to the car, nor did black-hearted thoughts pervade my thinking as I stopped to admire the two rocks gingerly balanced at the trailhead—unperturbed in their fragile yet strong presence.

July 2019

CHAPTER 36

I Read the News Today

As I scrolled through the headlines today, I began humming the Beatles' song "A Day in the Life," the final song written by John Lennon and Paul McCartney for their iconic *Sgt. Pepper's Lonely Hearts Club Band* album.

Lennon's inspiration came from newspaper articles he'd read, while McCartney's came from memories of his youth. The creatively written combination of John's fictionalized present-day occurrences with reminiscences of Paul's youthful experiences led them both to believe "A Day in the Life" was one of their finest, if not their best, collaborations.

Rolling Stone agreed, and considered it to be the greatest Beatles' song, and number twenty-six on their list of "The 500 Greatest Songs of All Time."

The boys from Liverpool achieved greatness from modest if not troubled beginnings, and then sustained it through messy, often contentious, creative and personal bouts of ego and individual "demon" driven biases.

I read the news online today as I do every day. I approach this practice with a bit of Pollyannaish optimism seasoned with a Cinderella-like dose of reality. I move from wishful thinking—*may good will triumph over evil*—to *oh, boy, what a mess we and the world are in*—and finally to *why did I watch or read this?*

The stories rife with conflict, injustice, suffering, and calamity pull me in, and their depressing tone makes me clamor for a Higher Power or Creator-God whose existence would help me make sense of the chaos. I wonder why I am consistently drawn to the abundant cynical, depressing, negative stories rather than the scarce positive uplifting ones. Tales of war-ravaged lands, the spreading of disease, and the reporting of racial unrest captured my interest today more than the feel-good stories of a beached pod of dolphins being rescued, and those of humans caring for and being kind to each other.

Why, when I want the Buddhist word *mudita* (appreciative joy at the success and good fortune of others) to be my companion, does *schadenfreude* (taking pleasure in the misfortunes of others), if that's what it is, seem to drive my news interests?

It's not that simple. Though I don't consciously experience pleasure at others' suffering, I am drawn to the darkness in our shared world. Perhaps researchers are correct when they suggest we envision the world to be a more hopeful place than it is, and that suffering and darkness jump out at us, triggering our vigilance and protective wariness in spite of a conscious or unconscious rosy view of life.

The world is a messy place, but one in which triumph, greatness, and beauty emerge and thankfully surprise us. The Beatles' partnership often became mired in stifled voices, jealousies, and conflict, from which arose occasional groundbreaking compromise and rock 'n' roll greatness. The lyrics to "A Day in the Life" contain references to the darkness in the world, but the orchestral glissandos and final sustained piano chord soar with hope and energy.

I'll watch the news tonight, and wonder again why the good stories, the conflict and tension-free ones take a back seat. I'll think, *oh boy*, but stay tuned. My Cinderella yearnings for uplifting narratives—pumpkins become coaches and slippers find the right foot—will compete with watchful waiting, anticipating the gloomy, less hopeful tales. I much prefer having a background of lightness punctuated by bits of darkness than experiencing the opposite. It gives me hope for all of us.

March 2015

CHAPTER 37

MARK TWAIN GETS IT, BUT DO I?

I love the bizarre and unexpected ways in which my reading and meditation habits open the door to my soul.

The Decalogue, or the Ten Commandments as they're more commonly referred to, came to mind recently as I enjoyed reading random passages from Mark Twain's essays. I'll get to him in a moment, but first the twentieth chapter of Exodus, which is the second book of the Torah and the Old Testament, and whose author is presumed to be Moses.

They are commands to worship only God, honor one's parents, keep the Sabbath (a day of rest), and avoid idolatry, blasphemous language, murder, adultery, thievery, dishonesty, and covetous thoughts or behaviors (especially about your "neighbor"). Judaism and Christianity embrace these biblical tenets as the cornerstones for worship and living an ethical life. And now back to Mark Twain, the man William Faulkner referred to as the father of American literature. The author and humorist had just finished a lecture before an enthusiastic capacity crowd when he was approached by one of the front-row attendees. The well-dressed man, a wealthy and notoriously ruthless businessman, cornered him and declared: "Before I die, I mean to make a pilgrimage to the Holy Land. I will climb Mount Sinai and read the Ten Commandments aloud at the top of the mountain."

"I have a better idea," the great author replied. "You could stay home in Boston and keep them."[1]

There's no record, at least none I could discover, of what the prideful man's response was to the author's withering sarcasm. I suspect the man's hubris prevented him from taking in Mr. Twain's words, and that he kept his retirement plans in place.

I, however, found his response provocative and challenging. My retirement plans aren't set, but if they included a trip to the Holy Land and a visit to Mt. Sinai, a God-like proclamation from the summit would not be on the itinerary. My arrogance and pride find plenty of opportunities for expression elsewhere.

This short piece has been percolating in my soul since the New Year began, already more than three weeks ago. Listing the Ten Commandments has been a doodling habit of mine during this time—an annoying one because the truths revealed make me uncomfortable, even as I smile at the design of my listings.

Mark Twain writes: "A man is never more truthful than when he acknowledges himself as a liar."[2] My aimless scribbling, however creative, exposed my propensity to lie to myself. In 2016, to the best of my truth-saying knowledge, I kept three of the Ten Commandments, selectively adhered to another three (when convenient), and broke four of them.

I took a modicum of solace knowing, in baseball, if a hitter over the course of his career gets a hit three out of ten times (.300) he's most likely going to end up in the Baseball Hall of Fame. In the statistically bound world of professional baseball, only one player has achieved a batting average of 1.000, and he was five for five but never played in another game due to a career-ending injury.

Though my love for the game of baseball and years of playing the sport never translated into Hall of Fame statistics at any level, for me success and failure, frustration and pleasure coexisted. With them came a desire to be better, a striving I now embrace on the spiritual playgrounds and fields where I roam, and life and God offer the same mix and opportunity.

However my Ten Commandments stats rise and fall in 2017, I will appreciate their ethical and spiritual values alongside Mark Twain's wonderful way of skewering arrogance, self-importance, and righteous adherence to anything etched in stone, including the Decalogue. As a devoted reader of his work and the Old Testament, I'll apply patience and humor, two great companions on the journey, while scrutinizing the stories I tell myself.

January 2017

CHAPTER 38

WHO'S GOING TO TELL?

Not me, I thought, *but who better than me to tell the elusive truth?*

"When you look at your face in the mirror, what do you see in it that you most like and what do you see in it that you most deplore?"[1] This is the second question Frederick Buechner suggests Christians ask during Lent as they attempt to discover "what it means to be themselves." For me, it is only slightly less powerful than the first question he poses about betting on God's existence.

Christian or non-Christian, regular mirror-checks— however disheartening, inflating, or truth-revealing—are good for our souls. That said, my initial response to reading his Lenten piece, this question in particular met with the disavowal: *There's nothing in this mirror image I either most like or most deplore.*

Check it out, I thought, *just in case,* and with coffee in hand, that's what I did, early one morning two weeks into Lent. Once the bathroom lights were on and the door closed, I faced the mirror. Beetlejuice, the Vermont version, glowered at me from the other side of the wash basin—a scary, disheveled mess. Two sips of coffee didn't stifle the keening howl I felt when the ghoulish creature with sprouts of unruly gray morning hair and sleep-encrusted eyes stared back at me. The a.m. stubble would be fashionable, masculine even, if it weren't for the fact hair follicles are scarce and hard to find on my right cheek. The symmetrical wrinkles, perhaps badges of successful aging, looked anything but that in the image facing me. They told a story I'd like to pretend wasn't mine: a map of bad-boy habits come home to roost.

Time to refill my cup with steaming coffee and my soul with cold, calculated denial. The latter was a tempting choice when confronted with discomforting truths.

And then, spurred on by a surprising dose of early morning courage, I looked in the mirror again, but closer and with scrutiny this time, taking in the reflection behind the messy finger smudge marks, dried water droplets from careless brushing and washing, and the streaks left when slapdash efforts to clean the surface were just that—hurried and slipshod. Digging further and peering even deeper into the familiar albeit distasteful image, I found what Buechner was alluding to—the most liked and deplored pieces beyond the messy surface.

In that spitting image dwelled a caring listener, a loving friend, and a disciplined pursuer of truth, all woven throughout the mind, heart, and soul of a conscientious seeker and reluctant disciple—a tough but gentle soul. There too was the countenance of a prideful man prone to churlish thoughts, self-righteousness, and self-conceit when life's path, events, and relationships didn't reveal themselves the way I wanted them to unfold, or when the universe didn't conform to my wants and wishes.

Seeing what I needed to see and not what I wanted to see was met with resistance and then acceptance, acknowledgment of both the deplorable and disheveled me as well as my soulful, caring self—the deplorably unkempt and the embraceable twin.

Looking beyond the well-ordered life I've constructed and with which I've been gifted means exposing and accepting the deplorable along with the most liked. Too often I've focused on riches, fame, (false) love, youth, and my health to define myself. William James dashes that focus when he writes: "Riches take wings; fame is a breath, love is a cheat; youth and health and pleasure vanish."[2] The American philosopher and psychologist also believed that "the art of being wise is the art of knowing what to overlook."[3]

However, we cannot overlook the things we don't know are there because we haven't taken the time to search. So we look in the mirror to find them, or life events force us to do so.

When my resistance prevents me from seeing naked truths about myself—the uncomfortable, deplorable truths—a beloved biblical character comes to mind: Jesus's disciple, Peter.

Peter was a rough-and-tumble type who often found himself in the Son of Man's disfavor for his impetuous statements and actions. On no occasion was this more evident than when Jesus, shortly before his betrayal and arrest, asked the disciples, "Who do you say I am?"

Peter, who had just finished leading them in a robust version of their favorite hymn, replied, "The Messiah!"

Bless his human soul. Like scores of others, Peter wanted Jesus to storm Jerusalem and throw out the Romans, then call down armed heavenly hosts to destroy the oppressors. When Jesus revealed what was actually going to occur—his own betrayal, arrest, mock trial, death sentence, crucifixion, and resurrection—Peter would have none of it, especially when his Lord and master informed him "today—yes, tonight—before the rooster crows twice you yourself will disown me three times"(Mark 14:30 NIV).

Only Peter, among the disciples, had the bluster and grandiosity to pull off what followed. He clenched his fists, raised them heavenward, and began to rebuke Jesus for his misguided thinking. "Even if I have to die with you," he declared, "I will never disown you!" (Mark 14:31 NIV).

Familiar with his beloved disciple's rants and posturing, Jesus said in a firm but loving tone, "Get thee behind me,

Satan!" Peter, sensing Jesus's displeasure with his antics, put the kibosh on his boastful enthusiasm, but not before he drew a sword and struck the servant of the high priest, the one who'd come to arrest Jesus, cutting off his ear.

Jesus knew patience even as he was all too aware of what lay ahead. Peter, the willful and impulsive disciple, is the one about whom Jesus said, "And now I'm going to tell you who you are, *really* are. You are Peter, a rock. This is the rock on which I will put together my church, a church so expansive with energy that not even the gates of hell will be able to keep it out" (Matthew 16:18–19 MSG).

Jesus healed the servant's ear, and later that night Peter denied his master three times. He'd been unable, or refused, to see himself through the mirror of Jesus's words. As the pain and hurt of his actions became known to him, he felt the wretchedness of his choices, his deplorable self, but he recovered and went on to fulfill Jesus's promise about the church. He became the bishop of Rome and, some claim, the first pope. He found a way to see beyond the self-serving image, the one we all can too easily embrace as the whole truth.

Peter is a kinsman of mine with whom I share the distressing trait of seeing what I want to see and disavowing what doesn't fit my perception of how life is to be. Though less rough-and-tumble than Peter (and I've never brandished a sword), my thoughts and actions more often reflect what I want rather than what a consistent follower of Jesus might do.

The acronym WWJD (What Would Jesus Do?) is a question I frequently pose during challenging moments. When I look in the mirror, only to see the disheveled Beetlejuice Roger staring back at me, my faith is buoyed as I ask, "What would Jesus do?"

March 2018

CHAPTER 39

ALL DAY AND NIGHT THE FROGS SING

Today is March 14. The outside temperature currently registers fifty-five degrees, which suggests either a cruel seduction by Mother Nature or a bankable harbinger that springtime is close. I'm imagining the verdant days of spring when birds delight us with song, and the frogs, peepers, and bullfrogs thrill me with their jazzy improvisations. Cold and dormant for months, the latter come to life, their outside bodies no longer frozen, and seek each other with robust serenading.

For months, perhaps a year, maybe even longer, I too have felt frozen and found none of the exciting challenges, stimulation, and exhilaration of my therapy practice carrying over into my personal life.

Can a successful psychotherapist struggle and be unhappy in his life while engaged in valued work with intriguing, exciting clients? *Of course*, I think. *Just not me.*

I'm desperately missing fun in my life.

Should I be writing this, making these thoughts public? I wonder.

"Write naked," claims author Denis Johnson. "That means to write what you would never say. Write in blood. As if ink is so precious you can't waste it. Write in exile, as if you are never going to get home again, and you have to call back every detail."[1]

Though trying, Denis, I'm not there—yet—not hedging, just scared.

During the month of January, there were nights, sleeping alone in a guest bedroom, when the German/Yiddish phrase *Bist du verklempt?* (Are you overwhelmed?) trolled its way into my consciousness and awakened me. In its wake, I became choked up, overcome with emotion, and unable to speak as I lay in the dark. A three a.m. snack and glass of milk, comfort food for my troubled soul, didn't help. Nor did writing in my bedside journal: "Life can be difficult, and living fully isn't an easy task, just keep on truckin'."

When desired solitude—sought-after moments of reflection and conversations with the God in whom I believe but too often find elusive—result in soul-crushing doubt, work becomes my mistress and lifeline.

I've often searched the Psalms seeking encouraging words from a kindred spirit, David, a flawed man of both wavering and grounded faith. His poetic voice gives me hope when he writes: "Cleanse me with hyssop, and I will be clean; wash me, and I will be whiter than snow. Let me hear joy and gladness; let the bones you have crushed rejoice" (Psalm 51:7–8 NIV).

Bruno Bettelheim writes in *Freud and Man's Soul:*

> The good life, in Freud's view, is one that is full of meaning through the lasting, sustaining, mutually gratifying relations we are able to establish with those we love, and through the satisfaction we derive from knowing that we are engaged in work that helps us and others to have a better life. A good life denies neither its real and often painful difficulties nor the dark aspects of our psyche; rather, it is a life in which our hardships are not permitted to engulf us in despair, and our dark impulses are not allowed to draw us into their chaotic and often destructive orbit.[2]

I am struggling to find this sweet spot—the one in which meaningful work and gratifying relations bring about a fully lived "good life."

The Psalmist's laments, often decrying God's silence and absence, are followed by words of adoration for God and renewed hope for his human and tattered soul. I find respite, a brief patch of well-being and hope in the cycle of his suffering and subsequent adoration. For me this also becomes akin to Freud's "good life."

"If I were God," writes my good friend and still-loving first wife, "I'd say to you, 'Lighten up and have some fun.'"

In response to her keen and light-hearted comment, I dig through the ordered stack of black T-shirts I keep in an upper drawer in my bedroom dresser. Though rarely worn, I find the one I'm looking for. The colors of neon green frogs have faded, as have those of the lily pads from which they're leaping, but the caption below them remains vibrant: "Time's fun when you're having flies."

All day and night, the frogs sing.

Time for a change of wardrobe. And some long overdue fun.

March 2019

–PART 8–

SPIRITUAL GRACE IN THE MIDST OF HUMAN MESSINESS

CHAPTER 40

BEATI IMMACULATE

While sitting in church, half-heartedly attending to the liturgy, my ever-curious meandering mind free-associated to fantasies both secular and spiritual. My wanderings were reined in by the Psalmist's words, and their unexpected confluence with the thoughts of a former counselee.

My memory of MJ (not his real initials) remains colorful. I met him when he was a sophomore at the high school where I'd taken a position as a school-based clinician. EmJay, that's how his mother told him to spell his name, "more sophisticated than MJ," she'd said, and that's what he did, obey her wish—an act of obedience foreign to him in most of the other areas and relationships in his life. His foul language and quick temper got him into trouble with teachers and peers alike.

After two years of working together, without much progress, or so I thought, he named my office couch the "EmJay Memorial Couch," then proudly declared aside from his mother, I was the only person "whose opinion he cared about, and the only man he'd listen to." He bragged, to anyone who'd listen that the only things in life he did more often than talk with me were to think about girls, drink Mountain Dew, smoke cigarettes, and fight—four habits for which he had an insatiable appetite. His self-declared white-trash upbringing made him "tougher 'n nails," he liked to say.

It was at this point in the worship service, the Psalmist's words injected themselves into my thoughts.

"Blessed are those whose ways are blameless" (Psalm 119:1 NIV) is the opening line of Psalm 119, the lengthiest of the Psalms, and the longest chapter in the Bible. In the Hebrew Torah, the opening words of the chapter, "*Ashrei temimei derecho,*" mean "Happy are those whose way is perfect," and the Latin phrase—*Beati immaculate*—refers to the first eight verses of the lengthy psalm, which read as follows in Eugene H. Peterson's transliteration—*The Message*:

> You're blessed when you stay on course,
> walking steadily on the road revealed by GOD.
> You're blessed when you follow his directions,
> doing your best to find him.
> That's right—you don't go off on your own;
> you walk straight along the road he set.
> You, GOD, prescribed the right way to live;
> now you expect us to live it.
> Oh, that my steps might be steady,
> keeping to the course you set;
> Then I'd never have any regrets
> in comparing my life with your counsel.
> I thank you for speaking straight from your heart;
> I learn the pattern of your righteous ways.
> I'm going to do what you tell me to do;
> don't ever walk off and leave me. (Psalm 119:1–8 MSG)

I'm certain when I knew EmJay he had no familiarity with the Psalm or the Psalmist, but on this particular Sunday, the sixth Sunday after the Epiphany, I wasn't surprised by the convergence of my memories of him with the Psalmist's lyrics. I recalled the February afternoon, ten years before, when he begged me to give him a ride home after school, a request which had less to do with our relationship than it did with my means of transportation—a fast and beautiful Porsche 911. He buckled up, his face flush with adolescent excitement and a macho "look-at-me" stare he made sure classmates saw—especially those waiting for their buses in the driving snow.

The roads were slippery, and in spite of his urging to "let 'er rip," I kept a slow, calculated pace as we traveled along isolated roads toward the trailer park where he lived with his mother and five siblings.

At the crest of a knoll, two miles from his home, I lost control of the car, and we went into a 360-degree slide down the middle of the two-lane road. When we came to a stop, I leaned over and asked how he was. All the brazenness and tough guy stance had left him. In place of the wiry fighter was a shaking, ashen-faced, speechless sixteen-year-old young man. The silence lasted a minute or so, long enough for snow to cover the windshield, and for EmJay to know his Porsche-riding days were done. "I can walk from here," he said and exited the car.

I don't know anyone who fits the Psalmist's description of being blameless, those "who never do any wrong," or in the Hebrew translation, "those whose way is perfect," and I suspect neither did the author of these verses. I know flawed folk who strive mightily to get it right, and good ones whose flaws, unannounced, bite them in the butt.

Several months after the winter spinout, I drove EmJay to Fletcher Allen Hospital in nearby Burlington to visit his beloved and dying grandfather. On that drive, his rage, created and nurtured by a life of isolation, brokenness, and poverty, exploded in streams of homophobic and racial epithets which I had never tolerated during our times together. I threatened to turn back if he didn't stop, and when he paused to consider my warning, I posed a hypothetical scenario to him. I asked what he'd do if a gay couple had spun off the road, as we almost did months ago, and got stuck in a snowbank. Without hesitation or hateful comment, he declared he'd help dig them out and make sure they were all right.

"But these are people you hate," I said. "Why would you assist them?"

"I don't know," he replied. "I just would."

Perhaps EmJay's response may have been an example of "Vermonter ethos," a culture of community transcending the awfulness of inbred bigotry and hate. However accurate that may be, I believe there's more to it. He didn't want to talk about why he'd help, and I wisely didn't probe, but I suspected beneath the palpable anger and fear was a wellspring of sadness, a feeling capable of generating empathy and generosity.

What was apparent to my meandering soul on this Sunday was how the Psalmist gives hope, and the memories of an angry young man remind me how multifaceted we human beings are—capable of being tough and tender, embracing and hateful, defiled and blameless—and, even if we live fully, the perfection for which we strive will always elude us.

February 2017

CHAPTER 41

TEARS AND LAUGHTER

"And if I laugh at any mortal thing, 'tis that I may not weep."[1]

Don could be stubborn. We'd met at the Crescenta-Cañada YMCA in California, where we became teammates or opponents during noontime pickup basketball games. Attendance at the competitive midday games evolved over time—players moved, job demands changed, interest waned, other sports or forms of exercise took precedence, and though I noticed his absence, there was nothing unusual about it.

Six or seven years went by, and my spiritual quest brought me to a nearby La Cañada church where he was a staff member. We reconnected during coffee hour following a Sunday morning worship service. Though it was obvious from his rigid movements and tremors something was terribly wrong, he spoke without bitterness about having been diagnosed with Parkinson's disease and the subsequent need to drop out of the pickup basketball games. He credited not only the practice of discipline in athletics, but also a tenacious commitment to an unwavering faith in God for sustaining him when the diagnosis could have ripped apart the fabric of his life.

I asked him how this could be so, to which he smiled and said, "I'm stubborn," and suggested we meet for lunch.

During the ensuing two years, he and I met once a week. I'd pick up lunch at a sandwich shop, bring it to his office, and we'd talk. Many moments of tears and laughter punctuated our discussion about faith and life events.

One of those luncheon meetings has remained a fixture in my mind. Don had asked me to pick up a turkey-avocado-bacon sandwich for him. As he patiently, but with gnawing hunger, unwrapped his lunch, I saw tears begin to roll down his cheeks. He was drenched in sweat, exhausted from the focus and discipline required for the most pedestrian activities, like unwrapping the wax paper and aluminum foil coverings and then positioning the much-desired sandwich for the first bite.

I asked if I could help, something he'd allowed on numerous other occasions. This time, he looked up from the disheveled mix of wax paper, aluminum foil, and what had been a well-constructed sandwich, and in a bit of irony, he shook his head, not in answer to my question, but because he'd begun to shake with laughter.

The mix of tears and laughter became contagious, conversation ceased, our shared interest in lunch waned, and we sat in each other's tear-filled presence as sorrow and joy unabashedly crossed the line from one to the other. Finally, taxed by the emotional outburst, we sat in silence. Don, still starving, took a deep breath and declared, "God does have a sense of humor!" Then with head bowed, he offered grace and began to pick at the broken sandwich spread out on his lap.

"Man is the only animal that laughs and weeps; for he is the only animal that is struck with the difference between what things are, and what they ought to be," wrote William Hazlitt.[2]

Within months of that luncheon meeting in 1990, my brother, mother, and I stood at my father's hospital bedside while he gave us his wish list for songs and Scriptures to be read at his memorial service. The treatment for multiple myeloma had not stopped the progression of the disease, and he was being sent home to hospice care with the expectation he would have a week, at most, before succumbing to bone cancer.

Alfred, my father, loved playing the piano and singing the hymns which had been a cornerstone of his faith and worship. He carried a sadness in his soul, one about which he never spoke, as well as an exuberance that would frequently make him break out in song. His exuberant, spontaneous singing often embarrassed me with the unchained scope and wavering pitch of his vibrato. As an adolescent, I'd cringe—a response I now realize was a function of my age more than of his voice.

For our visit to the hospital room, which my father shared with a fellow patient, we brought a Methodist hymnal and a King James Version of the Bible—both his favorites.

We were a wary and anxious threesome. I hadn't shared the recent experience with my friend Don, but as the three of us walked down the corridor to my father's room, I recalled the words of Mark Twain: "Against the assault of Laughter nothing can stand."[3]

Both my father and his roommate were afflicted with a terminal disease and were being sedated for pain. When we approached my father's bed, our mother bent down and kissed his forehead. His eyes opened, he smiled, and my brother and I in turn embraced him and gently stroked his cheek. All four of us were feeling vulnerable, but tearfully settled into chairs and began taking notes on my father's wishes for the service. We shared some dark humor—jokes about death, Mother's eventual remarriage to a man of great wealth, and questions about heavenly cuisine, such as whether shredded wheat, Alfred's favorite cereal, would be available.

When he opened the hymnal and began thumbing through its well-worn pages, he would stop, hum a familiar melody, and encourage my mother to join in. And then without warning or concern, he burst into song—"A Mighty Fortress Is Our God," as I recall. He closed his eyes, and in an instant, the small hospital room was his concert hall, barely containing the soulful lyrics and melody let alone his now unleashed octave-wide vibrato. His roommate must have pushed the call button, because within minutes the friendly charge nurse appeared and went to his bedside. My father continued to sing while the three of us smiled, shrugged, and looked at each other.

With a voice driven by desperation and a forcefulness which soared above my father's singing, his roommate exclaimed, "Get me out of here!"

The nurse was gentle and firm with my father, requesting he lower his singing volume, which he did, and then we resumed planning.

My father's room was on the eighth floor, and as we waited for the elevator to head home, tears flowing on all three of our cheeks, I began to laugh—not a gentle giggle, but a raucous, out-of-control belly laugh that triggered the same response in my brother and mother. We joined two puzzled occupants on the trip down to the lobby, but that didn't deter us. Our laughter increased in volume as we recited the man's words ("Get me out of here!"), mimicked Alfred's vibrato, and sang snippets of "A Mighty Fortress Is Our God" all the way to the ground floor, across the parking lot and into the car which would eventually take us home once the sobbing and laughter subsided.

My father died within days, and my friend Don passed away this month.

> God made both tears and laughter, and both for kind purposes; for as laughter enables mirth and surprise to breathe freely, so tears enable sorrow to vent itself patiently. Tears hinder sorrow from becoming despair and madness; and laughter is one of the privileges of reason, being confined to the human species.[4]

July 2017

CHAPTER 42

WRINKLES

Before we had wrinkles, we met in college, were in each other's weddings, trekked across the country on Amtrak, and hitchhiked with characters out of a Stephen King novel. Alan and I nurtured our friendship through grad school, career choices, the deaths of loved ones, and our persistent love for the Chicago Cubs—the core piece in our annual baseball junkets to various ballparks—which for twenty years began and ended with much-anticipated visits to "The Friendly Confines of Wrigley Field," home of our beloved Northsiders.

Alan and I spoke in February about taking our annual three-city trip to attend a series of baseball games. He'd been suffering from a deteriorating right hip, and when I asked about it, he insisted he could continue his busy travel and consulting schedule until after Thanksgiving, just as he assured me Tylenol and prescription meds would allow him to keep his commitment to the summer trip.

Tickets to six baseball games in three cities—Chicago, Minneapolis, and Milwaukee—were laid out on my desk, alongside JetBlue and Amtrak reservations. Reservations of hotel dates lay on Alan's desk awaiting confirmation.

Then in late June, one month before our twentieth annual summer baseball junket, I received a phone call which shocked and surprised me, though perhaps it shouldn't have.

"I can't do it," my close friend said. "The pain is excruciating."

"Our baseball trip?" I asked.

"Any travel," he replied, choked up and in a weak voice unfamiliar to me. "I'm housebound, crippled by the ceaseless pain."

The thin veil separating selfish from selfless in my soul, porous even when I'm fully conscious, vanished. My first thoughts, I'm ashamed to say, didn't involve sympathy for my friend's debilitating condition but instead consumed me with anger and disappointment.

I silently railed and cursed at him. *This should have been taken care of last spring when an opening for surgery was offered, one you turned down because you're so enamored with your overbooked travel schedule and presenting the image of being indomitable. We talked about this and you assured me the trip was on, and you'd manage the pain. You actually turned down my offer to postpone purchasing game and travel tickets because your tight schedule had only this one window available for baseball.*

Oh, my. And it went on in this way for another few seconds—mean and strident thoughts pushing aside the realities of his suffering.

You don't take care of yourself, and now I'm paying the price for your self-indulgent lifestyle. I've had two hip replacements and know the drill, but if only you'd listened to me. If only I hadn't bought into your assurance you'd be able to do this.

The rant continued to immerse me in self-righteous anger even as I heard his groans and shallow breathing. I didn't want to care, offer condolence, or ask how he felt. I knew better but didn't listen to myself—shame on me. His intractable pain and suffering coupled with the growing awareness of my self-centered and unacceptable thinking brought a welcome pause in our conversation. But then I began to hear my selfish inner thoughts, and in the judgment and sharp criticism, I heard the scolding, harsh voice of my mother and father, an unrelenting diatribe of how disappointing I was to them.

Mortified, I replied, "Let's take care of you first. What can I do to help?"

"I'm so sorry," he said through tears. "I blame myself for this, but I didn't want to disappoint you or myself."

We ended the call promising to reconnect the following day, giving both of us time to revisit the change in plans. During the ensuing twenty-four hours when I wasn't conjuring up plans to dissuade him—*we can use wheelchairs, stock up on pain meds,* arrogant me-first plot lines I acknowledged and resisted—I wrestled to prioritize what would be best for Alan.

When trapped in the murkiness of my dark side, I listen to soothing jazz. It is an attempt to improvise on the craziness in my soul. I close my eyes to look inside and get to know myself better. I listen, albeit reluctantly, to the voice I want no part of. I reach out to authors whose journeys parallel mine.

One such author, Saint Paul, whose words came to me later that night, wrote to friends in Rome: "I don't understand what I do. For what I want to do I do not do, but what I hate I do ... For I have the desire to do what is good, but I cannot carry it out. For I do not do the good I want, but the evil I do not want to do—this I keep doing. ... What a wretched man I am!" (Romans 7:15–24 NIV).

Bruno Bettelheim's book, *Freud and Man's Soul,* happened to be on my desk. Turning to the final chapter, I reread words I'd visited on just such occasions in the past when internal distress occupied my soul. The author recounts William Faulkner stating in his Nobel Prize acceptance speech "the problems of the human heart in conflict with itself ... alone can make good writing." Bettelheim carries the thought further when he states, "Freud took care to emphasize the conflicts within the soul, and their consequences for an individual—how he could live well with himself despite these conflicts—or possibly because of them, since they also make for the richness of his inner life."[1]

There can be no gain without loss, no light without darkness, and no yes without no.

The next day Alan and I talked again.

He asked if in place of our defunct baseball trip, I'd be willing to spend that time in Florida taking care of him at their seaside condo. Sara, his wife, had urgent commitments in Michigan, and my presence would enable her to fulfill them. "I'll buy your tickets and placate some of my guilt," he offered, and we managed a brief laugh.

I agreed, and we both felt relief from the dark and stifling tethering to selfishness, guilt, judgmental thoughts, pride and vanity, and gratitude to have an unexpected and embraceable way into loving friendship. So began our alternate plans.

We could watch a few games on TV, make our own game fare, enjoy each other's company, perhaps talk about being fragile and vulnerable with each other, about love and friendship, sacrifice and suffering, and how adversity, when taken in stride, can facilitate change.

While awaiting the Houston-Tampa connecting flight, I thumbed through a journal I keep with less diligence than I like to admit, but there I discovered a Frederick Buechner quote: "For Jesus peace seems to have meant not the absence of struggle but the presence of love."[2]

Hope began to seep into the cracks in the darkness through Saint Paul, Faulkner, Freud, Jesus and Buechner. I was in good company.

I arrived in Sarasota two days after Alan was released from the hospital, a decision his surgeon agreed to if twenty-four-hour "watchful care" was available as needed. He assured his doc he'd be in competent hands—mine—but I was less confident. Alan had been offered the use of their neighbor's condominium, a larger and more spacious living area than his own home, and one which we turned into our own rehab unit.

During the next eight days, we relaxed together, celebrated his modest gains in mobility, self-care, and the gradual cessation of pain. Humor became our constant companion as we shuffled through the aisles of the Publix market, laughed to the point of tears at politicians' gaffes and the faux pas of humankind—our own in particular. On occasion, the simple tasks of normal hygiene required four hands. We ate well, imbibed with discretion, and shared an abundance of joy in Alan's physical healing. Disappointments and hope were embraced, not the least of which involved watching and rooting for our beloved (losing) Cubs from the friendly confines of a Sarasota condo and not in the stands at The Friendly Confines of Wrigley Field.

September 2018

CHAPTER 43

SAYING OR THINKING "I'M SORRY" WITH GENUINE GRACE

My parents taught me well—apologize when you've wronged another. Saying "I'm sorry" shows empathy and respect for the other. Though well-intended in theory, their practice emphasized a hierarchical aspect—child-to-parent apologies were encouraged if not expected, but rarely did they practice the reverse.

As I moved through adolescence and into adulthood, I reacted to this by frequently rebelling, withholding apologies when they were warranted. Overcoming that stubborn stance as I've aged has been difficult, as I've too often resisted being accountable, owning errors of judgment, and acknowledging I've committed harmful acts or spoken hurtful words.

Thinking *I'm sorry*, let alone saying it, doesn't come easily for me. My vain conceit and its self-righteousness resurfaced in a glaring, unexpected way several weeks ago while shopping at a local market on a dreary, rainy day.

After posting a blog on the website (*Phoneless, Fat, and Self-Righteous,* July 6, 2016), I'd naively thought the temptations of judgment and criticism had been excised from my soul, or at least been muted, and thought or voiced apologies would be more familiar responses to my blunders and errors of judgment.

They hadn't.

Unsightly and repulsive, I thought as I watched the customer in front of me unload his cart at check stand number three. It wasn't the many-sizes-too-small, sweat-stained T-shirt alone which caught my attention, but the rolls of fat protruding everywhere that etched the undesirable image in my mind. The obese man, elbows resting on the metal handle, had filled his cart with bags of Cheetos, potato chips and nachos, and several cases of Mountain Dew. And based on the number of frozen packages stacked to overflowing, I imagined Fat Boy Jr. Mini Ice Cream Sandwiches must have been on sale.

My vanity led to exclusive thinking, as in *I'm better than he is,* and *I'm okay, he's a mess.*

Most likely no one in the checkout line that rainy Saturday picked up on my better-than-thou attitude. Nor would they have known my subsequent embarrassment and private humiliation when my critical thoughts awakened the more forgiving part of my soul—a voice no less compelling.

This isn't easy for me to write.

Once again when I thought I'd "gotten it," I was reminded the work in progress that I am is just that, a work in progress.

The story of that Saturday continues. As I unloaded a variety of fresh fruits, vegetables and an assortment of lean meats and fresh salmon onto the conveyor belt—and did so with more than a bit of conceit—the thoughtful cashier asked if I had a supermarket identification number. I replied I did not. The grossly overweight customer, about to roll his cart toward the exit, stopped and waved in her direction. "Please, here's mine," he said with unexpected grace. "Use it, Rachel," then smiled at me.

"Thank you," I said sheepishly, smiling in return. Exiting the market, I felt the weight of my demeaning judgment and that customer's grace.

I'm sorry, I thought. *I know better.*

I adjusted the hood of my sweatshirt, hung my head

in disbelief at my dismissal of the thoughtful overweight customer, and walked toward the shelter of my Volvo. Before opening the driver's side rear door, I paused. What had been a drizzle became a downpour, creating an indecipherable mix of raindrops and tears which rolled down my cheeks. What I thought I'd left behind—a part of my humanness from which I'd been freed—remained in place.

Once seated behind the steering wheel, mind wandering and hidden from scurrying passersby, I thought of three events when the graciousness of others had left a lingering impression on me.

"*Undskyld!*" Ulla had said, after spilling orange marmalade on my shirt and pants while serving my brother and me breakfast. Ulla, the daughter of a Danish business associate of our father and our first and only au pair, wanted to learn English and so had come to live with us in Drammen, Norway. I remember her gracious apology, spoken in spontaneous Danish that I didn't understand, but her eyes and facial expression conveyed what her words could not. It was one of the few times I could remember when an elder apologized to me.

Madam Reid, an excellent and passionate high school French teacher, deserved a better student than I was willing to be. During the years when she brought passion and linguistic skills to the high school French classes in which I was enrolled, I merely coasted, settling for being a B student. She'd remind me of this not by lecturing or scolding, but by writing *Je regret et je suis desole, B-* (I regret and I'm sorry, B-) at the bottom of my papers and tests. She knew I could speak Norwegian and believed with more effort I could learn French as well, and her "I'm sorry" written next to the grade was her gracious way of letting me know she took my nonchalant approach to be partly her fault.

Louise Penny's intriguing Chief Inspector Gamache novels, set in the small town of Three Pines in French Quebec, Canada, have well-defined characters who often speak the phrases: *desole,* or *je suis desole.* When the Chief Inspector first mentioned *his* mentor's four statements which lead to wisdom—*I don't know. I need help. I was wrong. I'm sorry*—I became aware of how few times I admit to any of the four, and how often I believe I know, don't need help, am right, and have nothing for which to be sorry.[1]

This makes me wonder if I'm different from those who seek my assistance as a therapist. No, I am not. Admitting to not knowing, needing help, being wrong, and apologizing requires that we shed our defenses and find strength in being vulnerable—not an easy task when our emotional wounds demand protection.

The rain-splattered windshield blurred whatever transpired outside in the storm, but the memories brought clarity to my heavy heart. *Be more accepting and forgiving,* I thought. When I'm confronted by my human errors, I ought to take responsibility for harmful words, spoken or thought, and do so without too much self-judgment.

Once the key was turned, the engine sprang to life and the wipers cleared the windshield. Jesus's Sermon on the Mount came to mind as I looked at my face in the rearview mirror.

"Why do you look at the speck of sawdust in your brother's eye," he'd said, "and pay no attention to the plank in your own eye?" (Matthew 7:3 NIV).

For the moment the plank had disappeared, and the speck was visible. *Je suis desole*, Jesus. *Je suis un etre humain brise mais repentant* (I'm sorry, Jesus. I'm a broken but repentant human being.)

I shifted into reverse and backed out of the parking space.

February 2020

CHAPTER 44

Amazing Grace

Years ago, on a ski trip to Aspen, Colorado, The Great Mystery appeared to me. On the evening before the unexpected event, after a challenging day on the slopes of Aspen Highlands, I'd met and had a beer with the head of the ski school, who graciously invited me to ski with him the following day. A significant snowfall had begun, prompting his suggestion we meet the next morning at the base of the mountain and take the first chairlifts to the top of the mountain for a pristine powder run.

The following morning when I met him at the chairlift, there wasn't a cloud in sight except the low-hanging fog bank which obscured the peak—our destination. The air temperature had dropped. Wisps of clouds and dense fog began to come in, rolling past us and limiting visibility as we ascended the final stretch. There was no stillness in my soul, and I became lost in fear and doubt considering the unthinkable—riding the chair back down the uppermost slope and into the sunlight. And then from high above on the shrouded mountaintop, we heard the plaintive tones of a bagpipe.

At first the sounds were intermittent as the wind and moist air muffled them. And then he appeared off to our left, a lone piper perched on an outcropping playing a familiar tune—"Amazing Grace." Although I love the lyrics of "Be Still, My Soul" set to the music of Sibelius's "Finlandia," no song grips my soul and arouses my emotions the way "Amazing Grace" does. "And grace will lead me home …" is among the lines giving me hope during rough patches on my life journey.

Bagpipers playing it take my breath away.

Are we not, all of us, somewhere in our souls, broken, beset by emotional pain, and yearning to be healed, trying to find our way home?

Many have found the lyrics comforting in unbearable times—being lost, filled with fear, surrounded by "dangers, toils, and snares"—and then hope they will prevail through divine grace.

Civil War soldiers, on both sides of the conflict, were given copies of the hymn. The Cherokee sang the song for strength along the Trail of Tears. Blind Willie McTell, Georgia blues legend, wrote that "Amazing Grace" was "a tune they used to hum back in the days when they'd be picking cotton." During the civil rights movement and protests over the Vietnam War, the iconic hymn gave solace and strength to all who heard, hummed, or sang the verses.

Bill Moyers attended a performance at Lincoln Center and observed "… the audience consisted of Christians and non-Christians [noting] that it had an equal impact on everybody in attendance, unifying them."[1]

Oh, how sweet the sound.

As we stood preparing for the descent, the sounds of the bagpipe persisted and gave me the courage I thought I'd lost. Even now, I remember my companion's words.

"Gets me too," he shouted. "Every time."

And then we descended the mountain.

July 2017

—PART 9—

THE GREAT MYSTERY, GOD IN THE MYSTIFYING AND DISTRACTING DETAIL

CHAPTER 45

A TALE OF TWO PARTIES

This is a tale of two parties. The first one involved treats, and the other, though lacking the typical party staples of edible goodies and drink, did share what all parties have in common—human connection and celebration.

The first party, a much repeated one during my childhood, defined occasional post-dinner evenings with my father, mother, brother, and me. It began with an endearing sequence of events. My father would stop in the middle of whatever he was doing and stand up, or he'd enter a room unannounced, rub the palms of his hands together with glee, and then with great gusto proclaim, "Let's have a party!" It was the signal to gather all manner of treats, cookies, cake, milk, and coffee.

My mother loved to bake. Next to the overhead kitchen cabinet filled with spices, condiments, flour, and other baking necessities stood the party cabinet, my father's destination on those occasions. The three shelves were stacked with round and square tins filled with Norwegian sweets and more common cakes and cookies. Krumkake (waffle cookies), Kringle (sugar-coated almond cake), and butter cookies shared space with containers of brownies, chocolate chip, oatmeal, and peanut butter cookies. Each of the tins featured taped labels on their lids, descriptions of the contents in my mother's precise handwriting.

All three of us participated in emptying the cabinet, arranging plates and tins on the dining room table or TV trays. With music in the background or a favorite television show providing the setting for our family gatherings, a celebratory time of eating, laced with fun-loving ribbing about slow, questionable board game moves or sharing thoughts about "who done it" on *Perry Mason* ensued.

The second "party" occurred two weeks ago on an early Tuesday morning when an unexpected event caused a celebration of human connection which surprised and warmed my heart. It happened on the fifteen-minute drive to my annual dental hygienist appointment. While listening to "Life is a Carnival" by The Band, my favorite rock group, random thoughts of my father's enthusiasm and love for connection occurred to me—a welcome and spontaneous distraction from the thoughts which usually occur to me as, with monumental reluctance, I prep for having my teeth scaled and gums probed.

Keeping pace with the music, I accelerated to fifty miles per hour as the Volvo descended a short, steep hill heading north on Mt. Philo Road, the scenic rural road between North Ferrisburgh and my dentist's office in Shelburne, Vermont.

As I joined Rick Danko and Levon Helm in song, a loud bang interrupted my reverie. Certain I'd heard a pre-hunting season gunshot, I glanced to my right, then quickly out the driver's side window. Almost instantly, though, my attention and all my driving skills were forced to the road in front of me. My Volvo suddenly veered to the left, then slammed to the pavement as the shrill sound of metal on asphalt drowned out The Band. I gripped the steering wheel and applied the brakes, and though I didn't panic, my heart rate soared as the Volvo skidded across the pavement before coming to a jolting halt. I stepped out of the car, took several deep breaths and saw the cause of the loud bang and jarring end to my trip—the front left wheel was twisted perpendicular to the body of the car.

Once assured I had my wits about me, I returned to sit in the Volvo. I called the dentist's office to report I wouldn't be making my appointment. Moments later, a man arrived at my window, eyes like saucers, short of breath, and asked, "Are you all right?" He introduced himself as Brian, then added, "We heard the bang and saw you sliding down the road, and I ran out of the house." He pointed over his shoulder to the house set back from the southbound side of the road.

I gave him my name and said I was okay.

He mentioned his neighbor and friend lived across the road and he'd introduce us, because Ed was a mechanic and might be able to help. At Ed's house, we found him under the hood of a Subaru. Introductions took place, and we all shook hands and smiled as we broke a Centers for Disease Control guideline regarding contact during the 2020 coronavirus pandemic.

After explaining my problem, Ed thought I'd damaged and broken ball joints, a strut assembly and possibly the left front axle. He offered to work on the car but wouldn't be able to do so until the following Monday. "Check with your mechanic," he said. "If he can't repair it sooner and you can leave the car here, I'll get it fixed."

I called AAA, arranged for transportation to my mechanic, and said to Brian and Ed, "I appreciate what you two have done. You stopped what you were doing to help a stranger. In these trying times, you still came to my aid. Thank you."

I didn't need to spell out people were tense about this contagious virus, that they were practicing social distancing and understandably living in a culture of self-protection stoked by fear and distrust, and despite all that they still chose to assist me. I believe they understood what I meant by "trying times."

They both nodded and graciously acknowledged it was just what neighbors do for each other. This was part of the appeal of Vermont and how I imagined it to be before I ever moved here fourteen years ago. We said our goodbyes, but before he headed up his driveway, Brian reiterated his invitation to join his family for a cup of coffee or a cold drink while I waited for AAA to arrive. When I mentioned Mike, my wife's son, was on his way, he said, "He's welcome too."

I decided to wait at the car for the tow truck and Mike, and when the latter arrived moments later, I filled him in, and we decided he'd meet me later at my mechanic's garage.

Approximately fifty cars passed me as they headed north or south on Mt Philo Road. Of those, close to forty-five rolled down a car window and asked if I was okay or needed help. Never have I felt less alone.

When Stephen, the tow truck driver, pulled up in his flatbed truck he quickly assessed how best to cinch and pull the car onto the truck's platform. As the chains pulled the Volvo in place, he reminded me fixing the car was better than having to "fix" me. We smiled and from that moment until we arrived at Broderick's Automotive, we chatted about careers, the weather, and how the Vermont lifestyle suited both of us.

Relieved the only damage involved a repairable car, I nonetheless began to see the accident as a catalyst for something wonderful—a celebration of neighborliness, empathy, and kindness, and an unsolicited act of grace.

My father and I held differing opinions on many subjects, and often our heated discussions were akin to arguments waiting for a place to happen, and too often, happen they did. However, I never doubted his love for me, nor did I question his genuine kindness and joy during those moments of connection when he invited my mother, brother, and me to join him for a party.

On the way home from Broderick's with Mike, I looked across the Champlain Valley toward the Adirondack Mountains and reflected on those family parties and what had just transpired with complete strangers. It was a beautiful, clear September morning, and thoughts of The Great Mystery revealing its presence in unexpected ways brought a smile to my face. Carl Jung came to mind, too, or rather a saying he kept in his office flashed before me: "Bidden or not bidden, God is here."

So, let's have a party!

October 2020

CHAPTER 46

MONKEY AND THE GREAT MYSTERY

The sharp sound awakened me.

"You were snoring," the voice declared.

The copy of James Lee Burke's novel, *Jolie Blon's Bounce,* lay open at my feet where it had landed next to the right rocker of my rocking chair after falling from my lap. Aside from Mike's cat, Monkey, intent on cleaning himself and unfazed by the book's having crashed inches from his hindquarters, I was alone on the porch. A rambunctious chipmunk scurried among the hostas next to the kitchen walkway. It too appeared unaffected by the loud noise.

Strange, I thought.

"Are you there, Mike?" I asked, leaning forward to peer around the corner of the porch, hoping to see my wife's son. No one answered, and the walkway to the front door was clear.

"Please stop staring at me," I said to the taciturn cat, now occupied with his forepaws. I glanced over my right shoulder to see if anyone stood inside the screen door. The kitchen was empty. Monkey finished cleaning, stretched out on the wooden floor, closed his eyes, and seemed to pay me no heed.

"Did you know," the voice continued, "cats sleep between fifteen and twenty hours a day but even when they're in their deepest sleep, they can hear and smell. Amazing, isn't it?"

"Hello!" I shouted.

No one replied.

I picked up the book, opened to page 346, where I'd left off to nap before finishing the epilogue, and began reading.

"I could see Legion running through the woods toward the bay, hogs scattering around him" ...[1]

"Want to hear a joke?" the voice asked in a gentler tone.

I turned in the direction of the sound but heard only the familiar creaking of the empty twin rocking chair to my left as it rocked back and forth.

Shaking my head in disbelief, I returned to the book, but before doing so grabbed the chair's arm and stopped its movement.

"... a bolt of lightning struck the bay or the woods, I couldn't tell which ..."[2]

"It's short, funny, and I think you'll get a kick out of the punchline," the persistent but not visible voice said.

Okay, I can play this game too.

Turning toward Monkey, I said, "Are you talking to me?"

Mike's cat didn't budge, but someone chuckled behind my back. I spun around but once again came face-to-face with the metronome-like movement of the empty rocking chair. Though the voice was disconcerting and frustrating, I had a hunch I had become the butt of a well-designed prank. I smiled, then reopened the book, assured eventually the perpetrators would be revealed.

"There were no wounds in [Legion] Guidry's body. It looks like he was hit by lightning. His boots were blown off his feet ... Anyway, he didn't go out alone. He was [found] floating around with a bunch of dead pigs."[3]

I shut the book and closed my eyes to savor the writer's last scene before heading up to my second-floor office.

"He's an excellent writer, Mr. Burke, that is. Do you know who gave him the idea for Legion and the hogs?"

Though tempted to answer the question, I hesitated, then said, "I'm not biting."

"Okay, think about it for a few minutes, but before we get to your answer, which I know you'll guess, I'm beside myself with giddiness, because I want to tell you this joke, so here goes. Use your imagination. A state trooper has pulled over Father Hennessey, who's heading to a senior home for a pastoral visit."

The chuckling became a veiled giggle, but this time I located the sound coming from in front of me, near or at the base of the porch steps. Resisting the temptation to peek, I stubbornly kept my mouth shut and eyes closed. *I'll show them.*

The voice continued.

"Officer: Reverend, have you been drinking?

"Reverend: Just water, officer.

"Officer: Then why do I smell wine?

"Reverend: Good, he's done it again!'"

Demure giggling turned into thunderous rejoicing. The booming sound made me jump wide eyed from the rocking chair, only to be met by the source of the untethered merriment—the tiny, hyperactive chipmunk, now on hind legs and holding its belly, was doubled up in raucous laughter. I closed my eyes, then rubbed them, but when I opened them, the unrestrained rodent, defying logic, remained in place on the slate walkway.

"What do you think?"

As I turned in the direction of the voice, toward Monkey, out of the corner of my eye I caught movement. The chipmunk scurried across the driveway and disappeared under the woodpile.

"Am I dreaming?" I asked, staring at Monkey. "And, if not, are you ...?"

Monkey lay motionless. "Whether you are dreaming or not, I am who you think I am."

My heartbeat increased. I took a deep breath and looked over my left shoulder where the empty rocking chair had begun to rock back and forth once more.

"You might explain what's happening as a form of shapeshifting, but the Greeks knew it was 'the appearance of god,' and called it a theophany—heady stuff. I like to keep it simple." The voice occupied the empty seat, no doubt about it, and though wanting to say something, I was dumbstruck and unable to sort through the swirling thoughts which took my breath away.

"It is a bit much to take in. Moses felt the same way, as did Saul on the Damascus road before he became Paul, the renowned man of letters. Which reminds me of our Mr. Burke."

I started to speak but nothing came out.

"Son, you'll get your tongue back, don't be concerned, and for better or worse you'll find your speech. I've seen this so many times. However, I've got a point to make about your favorite author. Do you remember the story of the demon-possessed man at the cemetery in the Gardarenes?"

Though I remained puzzled and awestruck, a strange sense of assurance buoyed me as I replied I did recall Jesus's casting out the evil spirits.

"Matthew, Mark, and Luke all recount the strange tale, but in Mark and Luke's version, when Jesus asks the evil spirit its name it replies, 'Legion.' Then my Son casts the evil spirits into a herd of pigs who stampede down the hill to their demise in the lake."

I paused, then realized where the voice was going. "Are you suggesting James Lee Burke used the gospel writers' story in his scene where Legion Guidry and the hogs are struck by lightning and found dead in the water?"

"You'd have to ask Mr. Burke."

Realizing how unlikely it was such a meeting and conversation would occur, let alone the one in which I was currently engaged, I remained silent and thoughtful.

"I know what you're thinking," the voice continued with a chuckle, "but whatever else, remember Monkey, the wired chipmunk, and this empty rocking chair. Your Mr. Burke's character, Dave Robicheaux, ended the book's epilogue with this thought: "... I wonder if there is any way to adequately describe the folly that causes us to undo all the great gifts of both Earth and Heaven."[4]

No, there isn't.

The rocking chair stopped moving, Monkey raised his head and meowed, and a light breeze rippled through the hostas.

August 2020

CHAPTER 47

GOD'S IN THE GAP

Though I dozed off during the seventeen-minute rain delay in the seventh and final game of this year's World Series, I had no trouble waking up as the tarps were removed from the field and play resumed. I wasn't certain about the outcome, but I knew I wanted to view it all.

Less than a week later, I vowed to stay up on election night to view the results. My candidate, Bernie Sanders, had been defeated in the Democratic primary, and though I had misgivings—voting for the Republican alternative was untenable to me—I voted for the woman who defeated Bernie Sanders, Secretary of State Hillary Clinton. There was no rain delay on election night, and being certain of the outcome, I went to bed, hesitating only slightly when I thought, *What if?*

Before dawn, I discovered "what if" had occurred. Feelings of despair, disbelief, and fear filled me. How could Donald Trump, a man who'd spoken and promoted hateful rhetoric, have won? It felt as if democracy's very foundation trembled—was at risk of being undermined. With such thoughts, I fell back asleep and had a lustful and poignant dream set in the fields of a popular blueberry farm overlooking Lake Champlain.

"Go down the hill until you reach row seven," a woman with mesmerizing eyes said, pointing to her right. "You can begin there, but I would recommend walking the full length of the row to its farthest point and starting there."

"Thanks," I replied, repositioning the Oakley sunglasses from atop my head to the bridge of my sunburned nose. "I'm Roger," I said, extending my hand.

"And I'm Missy," the woman in my dream replied as her hand met mine. "Have you done this before?"

"No, it's my first time."

"The easiest way to do it is to tie this around your waist," she said, pointing to one of the pails which, like all the others, had a length of twine tied to its metal handle. "Here, let me show you," she volunteered, grabbing the pail and grasping the end of its attached twine in her two hands. Reaching around me from the rear, she began tying the twine's two ends together.

I could feel her body brush up against my T-shirt as she tightened the knot.

And then, in spite of my burgeoning titillation, I recalled the apostle Paul's words to Titus, one of his converts, as he encouraged him to do "say no to ungodliness and worldly passions"(Titus 2:12 NIV).

Paul's personal admonishment and instruction to Titus, memorized years before in daily vacation Bible school, caught me off guard.

Missy turned me around, then moved so close I felt her warm breath on my cheek. With deft hands she adjusted the twine so the pail hung several inches below my belt-buckle.

"There," she proclaimed, "now you look the part."

"Nicely done," I said. "I think you've done that before."

"Every time is a first," she replied. "I want our customers to have the best experience possible."

I touched my cheek and then the blue pail with its plastic bag insert, smiled at the attractive young woman, and walked away in the direction she'd suggested.

Some things never change, I thought, blushing with arousal, and looked across the field of blueberry bushes toward Lake Champlain and the distant blue haze covering the Adirondack Mountains. I walked to the end of row seven, where, as promised, I discovered bushes with gangly sagging branches filled with marble-sized berries.

God, please do not remain silent!

A crisp breeze promised a change in the weather as a cold front made its way across the Champlain Valley. I'd come to pray and converse with the God whose existence I question as much as I'd come to pick blueberries, and now, as is often the case when it comes to God and me, I was distracted and preoccupied by other thoughts—in this instance, Missy.

God sleeps when I need him the most, I thought, as lustful images of the attractive woman vied for my attention. Experiences of God are never this compelling. As I walked between the rows of bushes, my thoughts were drawn to her in such ways that thoughts of God's presence eluded me.

Two crows flew by prompting a hopeful recitation of Martin Luther's words: "You can't keep the birds from flying around your head, but you can keep them from nesting in your hair."[1] They offered little solace. I was alone with my fantasies.

"Roger!"

I turned toward the voice, hoping it was Missy. Row seven and the rows of blueberry bushes to my right and left were empty. My heart quickened and fear overcame me.

"Roger!" This time the voice was deeper, more resonant than the woman's in my fantasy.

"Where are you?" I anxiously cried out.

"I'm where I said I'd be."

I spun around in the opposite direction, spilling the paltry contents of my pail as I fell backward into the bushes.

"I came because you wanted to talk with me," the voice continued.

"Who are you?"

"I'm the one for whom you've been searching."

"You're ..."

"Yes, I am."

"But I don't see you."

"Look beyond the obvious, Roger. You'll find me in the dark as well as the light. I'm in the openings and empty places where discontinuity exists. There, I fill the gaps."

I regained my footing. There was no one in sight.

"Talk to me, Roger. I've missed you."

I awoke in a sweat. Later that day, as I acknowledged and put aside the arousing content of the dream, I began to explore the gaps in my provincial, if not myopic, way of viewing the world and God.

When despair, flickering moments of despondency, and loss of hope and faith in humankind and democracy grab me, I run from the darkness to the comfortable and known, the seductive world I orchestrate to feel better about myself. That world has lushness and is filled with fantasy which helps me deny what this election made clear—the rise of Donald J. Trump was made possible by people whose pain, anger, and hurt had eluded me. I now understand I'd been listening selectively to the voices which resonate with my positions, and not enough to those whose discontent and disenfranchisement occupy the dark places in the gaps.

November 2016

CHAPTER 48

I Am Too Alone in the World:
The Owl and the Rabbit

A dusting of new snow covered the ground, and the olive-green camo tarp covering the remaining cord of wood was being tested by gusts of wind. The day before, I had adjusted the bungee cords to secure the tarp, the corners of which now flapped wildly as another winter front approached. Two large pine trees, one on each side of the raised woodpile, retained pockets of snow from the previous storm. From the road, they appeared as sentinels appointed to stand guard beside the stack of hardwoods.

Within the stack and the undergirding pallets, a protected structure six feet in height, there resided rabbits, mice, chipmunks and squirrels, all vying for space in a natural tenement of sixteen-inch logs of elm, oak, and maple. The stack of wood reflected hours of work, and though I recognized my handiwork was utilitarian for me and critters in the forest, I felt separate from its creation. I took pride, flatlander that I am, in the symmetrical stacking of the wood, and my success in building the strong foundation of pallets and stone pavers on which it lay.

I thought of my father who committed to outdoor projects, ones he engaged in with little interest other than driven by necessity. The seasonal upkeep and yard work provided opportunities for him to wear tattered but still functional WWII army fatigues, gloves, short and long pants, knit cap, T-shirt, and when necessary a sweater and jacket—all in army issue olive-green. He'd been drafted into the army, served his country, but didn't see himself as an army guy—he wasn't a joiner, an organizational man. He and I shared this trait, one in which we would become part of something but never felt we belonged.

On those occasions when he would playfully engage me as his coworker, fulfilling the "honey-do" list given him by my mother, I would tag along as his five-year-old lieutenant, gladly taking orders. We'd rake and shovel together, hose off screens and storm windows, and though I thought he looked silly in his fatigues, I willingly held ladders and handed him tools on request. He was my Hero and Captain. We were a team.

And now, decades later, as I stood looking out at the woodpile from my second-floor home-office window, I smiled at the memory and vision of my father in his "dress" greens.

My brief reverie was interrupted by movement on the far side of the woodpile where a large rabbit emerged from the safety of the pallets and stack of wood. Unbeknownst to me and the rabbit, a motionless but vigilant horned owl, perched fifteen feet above ground, had been watching and waiting.

I felt the same queasiness in my stomach I'd experienced as a boy when wind gusts caused the ladder to sway while my father clung to the leaf-filled gutter he was cleaning. Within seconds, the beautiful, lethal bird swooped down, claws extended, and pounced upon the unsuspecting hare. The strong and determined bird lurched up and down sinking its talons deeper and deeper into the victim's neck and back as the rabbit tried to resist and escape. The flapping of the tarp muffled any sounds as I watched in horror and fascination while the helpless prey continued to struggle to free itself.

Once satisfied it had control, the owl attempted to fly off with the rabbit firmly clutched in its claws. Though strong and approximately two feet in height, the predator, unable to get off the ground, dragged the kill through leafless underbrush to a location behind a large elm tree. I had retrieved a pair of binoculars from an adjoining room, and as I focused on the base of the tree trunk, the owl peered out from behind and looked straight at me—a piece of the rabbit's flesh hanging from its beak.

I was a part of something natural, chaotic, and unsettling, but even more importantly, an uncomfortable feeling of separateness overcame me. My presence was more as an observer than a participant—a feeling I frequently experience in my connection with God.

For some reason this conjured an old memory of my brother, who often described his place at the dinner table when our parents would be quizzing, instructing, or lecturing me as a time when he felt like the fourth wheel on a tricycle.

Now I stood in my own home, looking into a forest on our property, at a woodpile of my own creation, and felt *I* didn't belong, or had no place in what had just unfolded—the fourth wheel on a tricycle—separate and alone.

July 2015

CHAPTER 49

I Am Too Alone in the World: Crazy for the Storm

The room was dark, illuminated only by the light of the full moon and its reflected brightness off the snow-covered landscape. Picture windows extending the length of the first floor of my parents' New Jersey hilltop home gave entrée to the moonlight which bathed the three open and adjoining rooms in peaceful stillness. Shadows stretched across the floor, an eerie sight dominated by the silhouette of my father who sat on the piano bench at their beloved Steinway grand piano.

In the distance, the frozen, snow-and-ice-covered Raritan River, a thin broken thread of white brilliance, snaked its way through darkened patches of forest. The lights of New Brunswick sparkled on this subfreezing December evening, the second day after my return from college for Christmas break.

It was late. Our tension-filled dinner had ended. My laments about an absent or elusive God had been met with critical words and rash judgments delivered in harsh tones, a diatribe leveled at me by my parents—unsolicited comments about my spiritual inadequacies. I sat still, unresponsive, the hurt and anger rendering me speechless. My brother and I had carried the residue of the rancorous words and our feelings to the safety of our respective bedrooms in the back of the house. Our mother, quietly seething, could be heard at the other end of the hallway, rustling about in the kitchen, puttering, cleaning up after having made much ado about a job she insisted on doing alone.

Moments later and restless, I was drawn back to the main part of the house by the sound of my father playing the piano. I stood in the entryway to what was fondly called the music room. He loved to play in the dark sitting before the keyboard, often with eyes closed, facing into a distant "land" only he could sense, passionately playing whatever private tune drove his fingers to touch the keys.

Our mother also played the piano, but she played "by the book," memorized notes from sheet music without improvisation, never venturing into the unknown of self-creation and extemporaneous never-to-be-repeated expressions. She would often chide my father for his unshackled riffs, and he would cease playing his magical, unscripted melodies and return to playing memorized hymns to please her.

Years after my father's death, she told me the story of the time he passionately gave her a soulful kiss, an intimate gesture she rebuffed and made him promise to never do again. Much as he played piano to suit her wishes, I believe he also acquiesced to her style of romantic intimacy. "I love you, Doe," was a frequent response to her requests, a declaration of capitulation and defeat as much as its intent—a statement of enduring love.

I had responded to his playing, but also wanted to say goodnight. Now, as I stood in the alcove, I saw him hunched over, his hands momentarily motionless on the keys. The silence was broken only by the sounds of his sobbing. I noticed, too, that the kitchen had grown quiet, and he sat alone. An air of resignation seeped into and through the darkened room. I watched as he lifted his head, the silhouette of his body outlined against the Raritan Valley. Did he have regrets as I had, remorse for unwarranted critique? I wondered if he and I shared unspoken hurt and pain, feelings he did not know how to access, let alone express to his son.

And then, as I continued to take him in, tears clouding my vision, he turned from the window, addressed the piano, straightened up ever so slightly, and began to play. In the place of muffled sobbing, there arose a sweet outpouring of blissful sounds, music which began to dissipate the heaviness that had permeated the evening. He played with abandon, following his soul's lead—a composition both melancholic and exuberant, spontaneous and freeing. I whispered good night, and then before turning to walk down the hallway, I said in a hushed voice, "God's voice is present in your music. Thank you, and I love you."

My father was passionate about much in life, but he was also stifled and inhibited, caught in a conundrum for which he had some responsibility. I was nineteen on that December evening, and didn't understand his sobbing and my response to it other than that I loved him.

Now, years later, I have a deeper understanding of that night. I too have lived a passion-filled life with stifling and inhibited periods for which I bear responsibility—I too know what it feels like to be "alone in the world."

July 2015

CHAPTER 50

ALL YOU NEED IS A GOOD STORY

This is why I weep
And my eyes overflow with tears.
No one is near to comfort me,
No one to restore my spirit.
My children are destitute
Because the enemy has prevailed.
(Lamentations 1:16 NIV).

The anonymous author of the Old Testament Book of Lamentations, whose laments over death and loss following the destruction of Jerusalem in 587 BC, speak to me in 2020 AD. Like many others who grieve and struggle in the throes of the Coronavirus pandemic and the systemic national issue of racism, I too am bereft.

However heartbroken and angry I am about ongoing racial injustice, people's inhumane treatment of fellow human beings, and how troubled I am by the widespread chaos and uncertainty while the world writhes in the grip of a deadly virus, I have hope our spirits will be restored.

Though vexed by newsfeeds showing the horrors of police brutality, reporting sky-rocketing numbers of the sick and dying, and providing platforms for self-promoting leaders who don't care about the wake of death and destruction their ineptness creates, I'll not concede the enemy has prevailed.

I pose the question: "Where are you, God?"

"Where are you, Roger?" comes the reply.

"I am here," I whisper. "Help."

Perplexed by my own "doom-scrolling," I vow to resist its seductive hold on me, and search for good news, a feel-good story in the midst of pandemonium.

Not long ago, help and buoyed hope arrived in the mail from California, a note from my friend Gary with a copy of the *Pasadena Weekly* in which an African American business owner was interviewed. Perry Bennett and his wife, Melanie, moved in 2004 from San Francisco to Southern California where they opened Perry's Joint Café on Lincoln Avenue in Altadena. The café is a favorite place for Gary and his wife, Helen, to eat, a fixture in the redeveloped neighborhood to the north of John Muir High School, and a place where I joined them for lunch on a recent trip to California. More on this in a moment, but first my brief history with Lincoln Avenue.

In 1970, when I lived in Pasadena to attend the Fuller Theological Seminary Graduate School of Psychology, my wife and I house-sat a home at the northernmost section of Lincoln Avenue. For the two months we lived there, I rode my motorcycle on city streets going to and from class, Lincoln Avenue being the most traveled among them. Several years later, and for three successive summers, I had a job driving a Coca-Cola delivery truck. Grocery stores, mom-and-pop markets, and liquor stores up and down Lincoln Avenue were on my route. When Perry and Melanie opened their café in 2004, I had an established psychotherapy practice in nearby La Cañada and also coached John Muir High School's varsity baseball team—a small world in which six degrees of separation isn't just a theory.

Perry serves great sandwiches, some of which are named after jazz artists, Chicken Mingus, The Tuna Simone, and the Max Roast. Others are light-hearted take-offs on well-known jazz songs: Tuna by Starlight, Pastrami, No-Chaser, and The Egg from Ipanema. They, among a variety of hotdog selections from cities like Chicago, New York, and Detroit, get rave reviews from neighbors and those who travel miles to enjoy the delicious fare.

Here's the feel-good piece of Perry's story. A decade ago, Perry committed to making a difference in his community, so he started a college scholarship fund to assist deserving John Muir High School grads. Proceeds from a one-day fundraiser, a single day's gross receipts, would be given to a selected student. Perry says it best: "... I knew this community needed something like this [the café and scholarship fund]," and to those who are beneficiaries of the scholarship he states, "This isn't for free. When you get in a position to do so, I need you to come back and find a kid to support."[1]

My treks along Lincoln Avenue in years past took me through blocks of destitution and run-down neighborhoods. Perry saw this when he arrived, and this was his response: "There wasn't a lot of light ... I needed people to have a different experience in coming to a black business. Also, I wanted young black people to see—I needed them to see—something different on a couple of different levels. Community first."[2]

Oh, yes, the world is a mess and my laments are unceasing, and too often the combination of both prevent me from taking in the "good news." I cannot wait for guidelines to change, the pandemic to be arrested and locked up, justice to rain upon us, but until then Perry's story, among others, gives me hope that small steps by big-hearted courageous people will make the necessary difference.

The prophet Isaiah (65:17–18 NIV) preceded Perry by thousands of years when he spoke for The Great Mystery and declared: "See here, I will create new heavens and a new earth. The former things will not be remembered, nor will they come to mind ... for I will create Jerusalem to be a delight, and its people a joy."

One step, no matter the size, makes a big difference. Thank you, Perry and Melanie, for getting the prophet's message by your "boots on the ground" efforts—and lest I forget, thank you too, Great Mystery.

July 2020

CHAPTER 51

A Good Way to Die

"There is no good way to die," God declared over the lunch he'd ordered for us from Langer's Delicatessen-Restaurant on South Alvarado in Los Angeles.

"Just miserable death," he continued, "which makes what's on the other side spectacular." Ever the observant one, he noticed my reluctance to eat while he was making pronouncements, *pontificating,* it seemed to me, and when I told him so, he scowled. I quickly took a large bite and began to chew with vigor, not wanting to incur either his wrath or a lecture.

"Birth, life, death, hell, and heaven," he proceeded, "are all part of the plan." He encouraged me to eat, not overthink, and enjoy the pastrami, swiss cheese, and coleslaw sandwich. "How do you like the double-baked Jewish rye?" he asked, "and what about their homemade Russian dressing?"

I nodded approval while wiping a smear of the latter from my cheek. His mischievous look was disarming, but when he licked his upper lip, my hands tightened around the sandwich.

"I've tried hard," he continued, shaking his head in divine embarrassment, "to get my heavenly staff of bakers and cooks to replicate Langer's number nineteen, but they can't."

I gave him a quizzical look. My mouth was full, but he knew.

"Yes," he exclaimed, "the one you're munching on this very minute!" He sheepishly mentioned Jesus may have told the staff that his father's docs had put him on a restricted diet—limits on salt and watch the calories. "However, occasionally I secretly order one directly from the deli," he whispered, "you won't tell my Son, will you?"

I shrugged my shoulders. *Me* tell *him*? I thought, and almost choked swallowing the last of the pickle.

"Of course, you," he impatiently responded, "and don't look so surprised, foolish child, you'll get in. After all," he barked, "we need psychotherapists in heaven, too—almighty, do we ever!"

"You're God," I bravely said.

"Duh," he replied.

I continued, albeit with considerable chagrin, to list his accomplishments (to his obvious delight), a lame prequel to my question.

"Can't you orchestrate a good way to die?"

Not one to shrink from the limelight, he began to recite the good deaths he'd brought about. Swallowing the last bite of my sandwich, I blurted out, "Yes, well and good, but what worked for Moses, Noah, and David isn't necessarily what'll work for Roger."

He didn't miss much, and scolded me for talking about myself in the third person as if a linguistic ploy could distance me from the inevitable—misery in dying.

And then he changed direction by gently proposing I could go to sleep and dream of blue-footed boobies.

What?

"The feathered kind, not the ones you pay to see at the 4 Play Gentlemen's Club in West LA," he was quick to say.

"You know about that?" I questioned.

He smiled, winked, and with measured fondness said, "Is there anything I don't know—or a place I haven't been?" He picked up right where he'd left off before I naively interrupted him. "You'll die peacefully in the wings of tropical goose-sized birds. That's the best I can do."

"When and where," I asked?

"TBD," he said and disappeared.

March 2019

CHAPTER 52

THE BAKER, THE TEACHER, THE PUPPY AND ME

Uffda has as many meanings as it does spellings—an expressive word my lips enjoy pronouncing regardless of the reason for its exhortation.

To stoic Norwegians, the expression signifies strong feelings—from abject despair to unbridled joy, from dejection to unabashed playfulness.

The picture on my computer is of a courageous and forlorn-looking puppy, a cute beagle carefully negotiating its way down a flight of stairs. If the creature could speak, it would say "woofda." When I look into its wide-as-saucers eyes, see its frustration and exhaustion, I declare, "That's uffda!"

My introduction to the word occurred when I was nine years old and living in Drammen, Norway, with my brother and parents. Elsa's Bakeri, a frequent stop on my way home from school, was a bakery owned by Elsa Nielsen, a Christian spinster, who married ingredients into mouthwatering pastries—delights our fellow congregants at the Methodist church believed had been *"Kysset av Gud!"* (Kissed by God). Though skolebrød (school bread), my favorite, provided many pleasure-filled uffda moments for me, I doubt its mouthwatering goodness made me more spiritual.

On one occasion, when Elsa's arms were wrapped around two trash bags, I surprised her, causing her to drop the bags.

"Uffda!" screamed our family friend as coffee grounds and eggshells spread across the floor. She turned toward me, saw *my* startled expression, then did as she'd always done. She reached into her baker's display case, removed a warm skolebrød, and while placing it and a napkin in my hand, she allayed my concern she'd sworn at me by introducing me to the meaning of uffda.

For a time, its use in place of real swear words gave me a pass with my parents, who disapproved of cursing in any language. I liberally used the word to my advantage in other settings as well—expressing chagrin at my mistakes and miscues or spontaneous joy for pleasure and success—all without fear of reprimand.

Later, in adolescence, a disturbing uffda moment occurred.

Mr. Vlosky, my high school driver's education instructor, was a humorless man—I thought—one who took himself and the course he taught too seriously. I, on the other hand, displayed arrogance and disregard for the rules of the road and his instruction. He and his course were beneath me. One day, during a behind-the-wheel session, I decided to show my disdain for both by pressing the accelerator to the floor to pass a slow-moving trash truck on a steep hill. As our sluggish Ford crossed the double yellow lines, Mr. Vlosky jammed his foot on the passenger-side brake pedal. I yelled, "Uffda," and he shouted, "Pull over!"

"You don't have to like me or my class," he lectured in his high-pitched voice, "but you do need to obey the rules of the road, and I'll not tolerate foul language."

I deserved and received a D in his class.

Recently, while enjoying a quiet, scenic drive home from my Middlebury office, I pulled up behind a blue Subaru stopped at an intersection. Before the light turned green, my blissful gaze left the setting sun above the Adirondack Mountains to the license plate in front of me—UFFDA. I drove on and began to reminisce. Fond memories and an embarrassing experience occurred to me—warm pastries coupled with a single recollection of a bigoted high schooler, who thought he was better than his Polish driver's-education teacher.

I smiled as enjoyable, kaleidoscopic thoughts of school days in Norway captured my attention. I thought of Elsa the baker, Mr. Vlosky the teacher, and the beleaguered, cute puppy whose quandary had captured my attention enough to make the snapshot one of the desktop background images on my computer.

Appreciating the importance of the moment more than the reality of it occurred to me as my eyes left the personalized plate to gaze upon the eastern slopes of the mountains.

Elsa baked fabulous pastries which, as my grandfather would say, tickled my palate. More, she was a caring soul who took an American boy in a strange, wonderful country under her wing, and made him—me—feel welcome.

Mr. Vlosky, who received the brunt of my bigotry and inexcusable self-importance, taught me more than how to drive a car. The lesson, on the surface, had to do with adhering to the rules of the road, but the importance of the moment was that crossing lines into mean prejudice had no place in my life. It took me until the week before my high school graduation to recognize it and summon the courage to face him, but I did. He graciously accepted my apology, and then to my surprise extended his hand and said, "Uffda, you've passed a bigger test."

I'm guessing the beguiling puppy in the snapshot I saved on my desktop found its way down the stairwell and learned about both reality and the importance of the moment.

Uffda!—a reminder of Tolkien's words: " ... not all those who wander are lost."[1]

There are times in my life when I falter, get in over my head, and make and acknowledge egregious mistakes, only to cry out "Uffda!" Then with perseverance (whose source often baffles me) and hope (equally puzzling), I resume the journey to arrive at my destination proclaiming, "Uffda!" Or as Strider (*Lord of the Rings*) jubilantly proclaimed: "A light from the shadows shall spring!"[2]

Perhaps God smiles, and whispers: "Amen."

June 2017

—PART 10—

TALES FROM ADVENT

CHAPTER 53

ADVENT AND THE POWER AND THE GLORY

There are no such things as normal people. I am in good company.

Which brings me to the celebration of my seventy-fourth Advent. During the first ten, I had guileless innocence for a companion, but the last sixty-four have been fraught with wavering belief and unbelief in the virgin birth, and doubt and questioning about the other subsequent mysterious and compelling tales about the man, Jesus, God's Son incarnate, whose life began as a babe born to a virgin in a Bethlehem manger.

Twenty-four hours before Thanksgiving Day, and four days before the first Sunday of Advent 2019, two events occurred: I became sick with a yucky "woe-is-me" cold-and-flu combination and had a vibrant dream in which I sat on the piano bench next to Rick Blaine, and Sam, his pianist, smoked a Chesterfield and sipped whiskey in Rick's Café in Casablanca.

The non-life-threatening illness caused weight loss, misery, exhaustion, and days of feeling fragile and vulnerable in my weakened state. In the dream, Rick uttered one of the movie's famous lines: "Of all the gin joints, in all the towns, in all the world, she walks into mine. Play it, Sam. Play 'As Time Goes By.'"[1]

During Advent, restless faith and reluctant discipleship notwithstanding, I read Matthew 1:18 through Matthew 2:12, the tax collecting apostle's account of Jesus's birth. Other stories—*The Gift of the Magi* by O. Henry, about personal sacrifice for those we love; *The Fir Tree* by H. C. Andersen, encouraging embrace of the present over focus on the future; *The Night Before Christmas* by C. Moore, regarding childlike hope; and Charles Dickens's *A Christmas Carol*, about suffocating bitterness turning into freeing love—all these play a role in my annual Advent reading list.

But this year, the Thanksgiving eve dream and Rick's words from the movie haunted me, and as I sniffled and coughed and sought bellyache relief, I wondered if there could be an interpretation of the dream I was missing.

The morning of the first Sunday of Advent arrived. Predawn chills failed to keep me between the sheets as I felt compelled to search for new Advent reading. Scanning the bookshelf in front of my desk, my eyes lit upon the book I'd been promising myself to reread for a dozen years, Graham Greene's masterpiece, *The Power and the Glory*.

Now suddenly, my dream made sense. Rick Blaine's reference to gin joints resonated with my library of books, among which was one which had been "seeking" me and from which I'd hidden for twelve years, the story of the whiskey priest.

Why now? I questioned. The answer, I knew, lay hidden in the narrative of the hunted priest who steadfastly pursues his sacramental duties as a fully fallible human being.

The questioning turned to apathetic reading as I struggled through part one of the novel, frequently dozing off, having to reread glazed-over paragraphs while wondering if there might not have been good reason why I hadn't revisited Greene's classic.

Stories about a curmudgeonly old employer, Santa preparing to descend a chimney, a misguided fir tree, and children exchanging gifts took on renewed interest. My friend and editor, Herta, encouraged me: "Oh no, don't stop, it's a wonderful story, an engrossing classic. Keep at it!"

I did.

At some point, and it matters not when or at what scene in the hunted priest's travels and travails, I became his companion, an uncertain, questioning human being attempting to find and embrace a spiritual Mystery, truth beyond gratitude for nature's granting my birth, and owing nature my immanent death.

That first Advent week involved not only parceling out over-the-counter meds for congestion, a runny nose, elderberry lozenges for unexpected spates of coughing, but also one in which I didn't want my fictitious companion's journey to end, and so I rationed daily readings based on his days of travel and sleep.

When the whiskey priest's story ended in his death, an inevitable outcome, his commitment to the God of his calling stayed with me. Though he had broken the vow of celibacy by having a mistress and fathering a daughter, and consistently flouted the laws of the land, he remained, to his last breath, a searching follower of God's Son, the babe born of a virgin. When his prayers seemed hollow, he found grace and God's presence in the Eucharist, the bread and wine bringing his faith alive.

His story, read this early Advent period, gives me hope as I fumble my way physically and spiritually into another season of Advent. Theologian Dietrich Bonhoeffer wrote, "The coming of God (Advent) is truly not only glad tidings, but first frightening news for anyone who has a conscience ... (Jesus will) confront you in every person that you meet."[2]

Reuniting with the whiskey priest again, but really for the first time, attests to me of the truth in Bonhoeffer's words.

And now, as I shuffle among Christmas stories, the comfortable and familiar ones I've grown fond of revisiting each year, I do so with the memory of the mule-riding, fallible, yet tenaciously spiritual, whiskey priest at my side.

And I am more assured than ever there are no normal people, and I am in good company as time goes by.

December 2019

CHAPTER 54

FINDING SOLACE

Raindrops obscured the bucolic view into the forest and my hopes for a better world, pelting against my home-office window like news releases of disaster and war which battered my soul and challenged my faith in God and man.

In desperation, I turned to a source where, in the past, this reluctant disciple has often found rekindled faith.

My uneasiness was not completely allayed by Frederick Buechner's words from his book, *The Clown in the Belfry,* though at first, a glimmer of hope emerged.

It was the first week of Advent, and I struggled to stay focused on hope, joy, and celebration as well as the "goodness" of humankind in a world where self-interest too often presides over community. The news was bleak, discouraging, and fraught with despair, my half-full cup draining into emptiness. And so I read from Buechner's book:

This story that faith tells in the fairytale language of faith is not just that God is, which God knows is a lot to swallow in itself much of the time, but that God comes. Comes here. 'In the great humility.' There is nothing much humbler than being born: naked, totally helpless, not much bigger than a loaf of bread. But with righteousness and faithfulness the girdle of his loins. And to us came. For us came.[1]

Am I embracing magical thinking, creating a narrative to find solace amid chaos?

"Is it true—not just the way fairy tales are true but as the truest of all truths? Almighty God, are you true?" Buechner writes.[2]

I have wrestled with this since childhood, and the flustering effect is endless. Drops of water slide down the windowpane, creating small streams which block my view, just as evil's presence in the world clouds our faith. Hope slips through our fingers, eluding our grasp.

Buechner goes on to say: "When you are standing up to your neck in darkness, how do you say Yes to that question? You say Yes, I suppose, the only way faith can ever say it if it is honest with itself. You say Yes with your fingers crossed. You say it with your heart in your mouth. Maybe that way we can say Yes."[3]

My eyes are closed, and though not yet there, I feel a shortness of breath as my steadily throbbing heart inches its way up my throat, but read on: "He visited us. The world has never been quite the same since. It is still a very dark world, in some ways darker than ever before, but the darkness is different because he keeps getting born into it."[4]

Will it snow soon, and coat the darkness in white?

"Anyone who has ever known him has known him perhaps better in the dark than anywhere else because it is in the dark where he seems to visit most often," Buechner says, as he writes for us all.[5]

The view into the forest from my window remains unchanged. The book has been returned to the shelf where it never gathers dust, and I reoccupy the seat at my desk—fingers crossed and heart in my mouth.

Advent has arrived.

December 2017

CHAPTER 55

MOSTLY NAUGHTY AND NICE

The phrase "naughty or nice" is seasonal, applying to children in particular, but after digging deeper I discovered the words described some of my year-round behaviors, and not just as a youngster. "Naughty" originally meant "not a whit," eventually evolving to *disobedient*. "Nice," surprisingly, meant stupid (one of my least favorite words) or ignorant. In my efforts to discover what makes me tick, I've embarrassingly found all four definitions have applied to me—a sort of gift I'd often like to leave wrapped and unopened under the tree.

The following two short tales involving mischief, mistakes, and misdemeanors fall under the category "Roger, what were you thinking?"

I wasn't, in either instance.

The first story takes place years ago on a sunny Saturday in December, when I met up with three seven-year-old buddies at the horse trough by Five Corners—the intersection of Farragut Avenue, Broadway (north), Broadway (south), Main Street, and Chauncey Lane—in our hometown, Hastings-on-Hudson. Three inches of snow had fallen during the night, making for great sledding, snowball fights, and boys-will-be-boys horseplay. After careening down a few nearby hills, we became restless for new adventure, stashed our sleds, crossed Five Corners, and with mischief in mind headed down Main Street into the center of town.

We teased, jostled, and threw snowballs at each other until we reached the five and dime store where our shared hunger for candy had us remove our gloves and search for the monies which would satisfy our cravings. We didn't have a penny among us. Bruce, Billy, or Johnny may have suggested it, but I think it was my idea to try our hand at shoplifting. The owner, a stern, unfriendly, and old bespectacled grump of a man rarely came out from behind the checkout counter. We mimicked him before and after making our frequent purchases.

I recall displaying a false bravado as I swaggered down the candy aisle while my friends hung around the Christmas decorations near the front counter. I filled my coat pockets with boxes of Good 'n Plenty and packages of Juicy Fruit gum, then headed back to the front of the store only to discover my friends had left and the owner, glasses perched on the bridge of his nose, was blocking the exit.

"What have you got in your pockets?" he asked.

"Nothing," I replied.

"They look pretty full to me," he responded. "Why don't you empty your pockets here?" he said, tapping his finger on the countertop. By this time all my swagger was gone, and I sheepishly obeyed his command. He reached behind the counter, retrieved his phone book, then slammed the phone book down in front of me. "What's your name?" he asked. I tried to pronounce it but hesitated as terror tightened its grip on me. "Speak up!" he shouted.

I stammered and identified myself as he licked his thumb and began paging through the directory. I could barely stand while he rustled through the book to the Ms, and then he shut the book and stared at me—a quaking, terrified squirt of a kid. He didn't waver and I didn't move. Finally, after what seemed forever, he picked up several of the packages of gum and boxes of candy, held them in front of me and said, "Merry Christmas, share these with your friends, and remember what happened here today. Now leave my store."

The next time I walked into his store, I was a senior in high school, and I was certain he recognized me even though he never said a word. I remember the feeling of being caught, the guilt, and the shame I experienced standing in the shopkeeper's presence. Some life lessons, however, require repetition (at least for me they do), and though I broke rules, told untruths, committed acts of mischief, and made mistakes, I wasn't tempted to shoplift again until years later when a graduate school classmate dared me to do so.

My wife and I lived in a small guest house in La Cañada, California, and we'd invited friends over for a Christmas party—a celebratory night of music, food and drink, and excellent weed. My wife was a high school teacher and I was pursuing a doctorate in psychology, two good reasons for me to mind my p's and q's, right?

Apparently not, because when we consumed the last of the Galliano we were using to make Harvey Wallbangers, a classmate and I drove to the nearby Ralph's Supermarket where I accepted his dare to shoplift a tall, gallon bottle of Galliano. It was close to midnight on a rainy December Saturday night, and I'd grabbed the first available coat—a black trench coat—from our small closet, a fortuitous choice if I were to successfully pull off the heist of the liqueur. Which, to my shame, I did.

The last of the guests left in the early morning hours, and did so without consuming more alcohol, choosing instead to satisfy their munchies by devouring all the festive Christmas cookies arrayed on the kitchen counter.

The attractive thirty-six-inch-tall bottle of Galliano remained upright and centurion-like in a corner of our tiny living room, a shopkeeper presence and reminder of a little boy's thievery that for three weeks wouldn't leave me be. Finally, guilt-ridden and shamed, I returned to the market on Christmas Eve, bottle unopened and openly displayed.

I walked over to Glen, the assistant manager and an acquaintance, and revealed my crime as well as my earlier shoplifting event. He smiled, accepted the bottle and my story, and then wished me a Merry Christmas.

"Do I owe you anything?" I asked.

"No, I think you've paid your dues. Enjoy the holidays."

In the years since, as in the ones before, I've been mischievous, made mistakes, and committed regrettable acts. Advent has been a celebratory time of year for me, a reflective period when reluctant accountability is mixed with hope for new beginnings. The gift of grace is not only present in the Christmas story, but in the recollections of forgiveness from an aging shopkeeper, an assistant store manager, and others who've made my bumpy journey less jarring.

Merry Christmas, and thank you.

December 2017

CHAPTER 56

CAROLS AND A BEATLES CHRISTMAS

I awoke from a good night's sleep, barely had my head off the pillow when King Solomon's words came to mind: "Meaningless! Meaningless! Says the Teacher. Utterly meaningless! Everything is meaningless. What do people gain from all their labors at which they toil under the sun?" (Ecclesiastes 1:1–3 NIV).

And that was just the beginning; a screed of negativity, judgment and criticism followed Solomon's words in my mind. *You're not good enough! Can't you do anything right! Why is he so oblivious? What gives her the right to treat me, or anyone like that? POTUS, politicians, harassment allegations, racism, rampant bad behavior, why? Really, you've got to be kidding, he said that! She did that, how could she? You can't be serious. You're joking, right? Can't we do better? Can I do better? I'm concerned, no, I'm worried. Actually, I need to get back in therapy; despair, my unwanted guest, is taking up residence!*

It's almost daybreak when I pour a second cup of coffee and head upstairs to my home- office.

For heaven's sake, I think, *the lurking shadows, castaway junk, all the "stuff" I work hard to eliminate from my life that still seeps and creeps into it, finding a place for its voice to get a hearing, a toehold en route to becoming a fixture, and during Advent no less. Whatever happened to Christmas?*

I'll not have this chatter. "Stop! Vamoose!" I declare in my loud outdoor voice, and with a smirk, I say, "God, where are you?"

And then the phone rings. I pick it up and my friend's wife Desley says, "I'm calling with the sad news that Don has passed away into his glory." In addition to the sadness, she feels relief her husband's suffering is over. I'm not surprised at either. He looked frail when my friends and I saw him Memorial Day Weekend, and both Don and Desley appeared exhausted.

We share a few memories, including his love of The Beatles. I offer condolences, and though she hasn't firmed up a date for the memorial service, she'll let me know when it's set, sometime in January, she thinks. Her voice is calm, suggesting gratitude, as she describes the final bedside moments of his life, filled with the voices of his beloved family members. They touched and held him, and spoke of their love and affection, while in the background the quiet sounds of The Beatles accompanied his parting.

I too am saddened by the news and relieved for Don and his family, but also surprised my kvetching and preoccupation with life's junk has been replaced by a desire to celebrate both the advent of new birth and the ending of a life well lived. The decision to enjoy and immerse myself in music, the gift my parents gave me when I was a child, is easy to make. Don's life will be celebrated, as I celebrate the birth of the Christ child, by playing The Beatles alongside Nate Cole, The Mormon Tabernacle Choir, Diana Krall, The Three Tenors, Mahalia Jackson, and Ray Charles, among others. I start humming "Joy to the World" mixed in "With A Little Help From My Friends"—music has chosen me, and our "dance" begins—a caroling Beatles Christmas.

"In My Life," from the album *Rubber Soul*, reminds me of the beautifully drawn words, *primum non nocere* (first, do no harm), that Don designed, mounted, and framed, and I hung in my office the first day I opened the practice. A triptych of medieval figures scurrying around in their villages, another of Don's marvelous drawings, hangs in front of me on the far wall. Don knew Ringo Starr's birth name was Richard Starkey before any of us knew who Ringo was—he was that kind of aficionado of their music and the Liverpool sound. In 1968, Don's and my first opportunity to vote in a presidential election, we took great pleasure in voting for the write-in candidate on the Freedom and Peace Party, Dick Gregory. Don was bright and witty, kind and gentle, and I am grateful for the musical sounds which stir my fond memories of him.

These memories during *this* Advent season are companion recollections to my own joy-filled childhood memories of Christmas when the sounds of Mario Lanza, the New York Philharmonic, Jussi Bjorling, and the London Symphony Orchestra, among others, filled our home with celebratory music as our family welcomed the celebration of the birth of Jesus. They are sweeping away the sense of meaninglessness and naysaying which almost hijacked my soul—a gift that keeps on giving.

John Lennon's lyrics from "In My Life" take on new meaning for me this season. He plaintively, but with joy, sings that he'll always have affection for the people and events from his past, keeping those memories close, while often pausing to savor them.

Merry Christmas.

December 2017

CHAPTER 57

THE LITTLE DRUMMER BOY'S GIFT

Billy didn't look up from his drum when his burly older brother, Thomas, barged into their shared room. Though deaf and mute since birth, Billy could sense the presence of others. It was one of his secrets.

Today, though, he had another secret.

"Working on your drum again, I see!" Thomas signed to Billy while shouting, "You playing for a King is a crazy idea. Mom and Dad think you're nuts too. Hearing voices telling you of wise men and a special baby born in a manger—what nonsense."

Neither his parents, nor his brother or sisters, knew of his plan to sneak out before dawn and follow the Magi's summons, his commitment to the six-mile walk from Jerusalem to the inn and manger in Bethlehem where he'd play for the newborn baby and his parents.

Thomas's sign language was sloppy, but Billy got the message. He wished he hadn't revealed the Magi dream to his parents, but it was too late now.

"They're tricksters," his brother continued. "If they even, you couldn't hear them. After all, you're deaf and dumb."

Billy knew what he could and couldn't hear, and what he chose not to see.

Thomas's taunting hurt, and though only six years old, he'd adapted to the ridiculing of his jealous siblings. Their stinging slights often brought tears to his eyes. He continued to stretch the goatskin across the wooden shell of his drum.

Known in the neighborhood as "that little drummer boy," Billy had a gift, a talent for playing drums, creating music which astounded and befuddled listeners. He played notes and tunes only he could hear, ones the Magi had heard as well, and who had therefore summoned him to follow their lead.

Dinner at dusk consisted of bread and olive oil, a few grapes for each, and a small piece of fish divided equally among them. Whatever fish Billy's father caught were sold at market, but on occasion he'd surprise them and bring home small tilapia to roast and serve with their staples.

Billy went to bed satisfied and full of excitement for the day and night which lay ahead. He barely slept and eventually stopped trying, slipped on his small robe, leather belt, and sandals. After hoisting his drum onto his back and tucking the drumsticks into a fold in his robe, he tiptoed from the hut.

Certain the music would be revealed to him, a mystery he embraced, he began his journey to Bethlehem. The sun rose and with it came the stifling heat. Sweat poured from his brow and blurred his vision, but he never lost sight of his commitment. At one point, while a flock of gulls flew overhead, he stopped under a fig tree, picked a few low-hanging figs and listened as a woodpecker pecked at a sycamore tree just off the path.

The simple pulsating beats began to create a melodic string of notes in his soul, a composition which brought a smile to his face and prompted him to start skipping along in unison. His lips moved, and though he couldn't hear himself moan and sing what his soul was composing, he could feel the rhythm reverberating in his head, exciting his lips and tongue to join his legs in an impromptu dance and chorus. He began moving his arms to the beat only he could hear—a dress rehearsal without sound, but one filled with joy and celebration.

There were hills to climb, vast stretches of desolate landscape to traverse, but Billy kept moving, swaying, and listening to the musical notes as they filled his time on the road. Other pilgrims, all heading in the opposite direction, waved as they passed, and some moved to the edge of the path, at first not knowing what to make of the strange little boy's dancing and singing. The little drummer boy was oblivious to their wariness, nor did he notice the passersby soon stopped, transfixed by his jubilant behavior. He danced and walked until the sun set, resting only to catch his breath and drink from the springs beside the road.

A lone bright star shone above the thatched roof of a large hut. Off to its side stood a small open structure, surrounded by a few cattle and sheep, a lamb, and three saddled camels. A single candle cast a shimmering light on the inside of the cramped structure.

This must be it.

He squinted and could see a young woman cradling a baby with a man standing beside them. Then he paused in the shadow of the large building.

Am I enough?

There were times, too many, he knew, when he resented how Thomas loved the sound of his own words. But now as he approached the dimly lit, hay-strewn hut and its occupants, he envied his brother's ability to hear his own voice.

The words of the Magi returned to him. "Come, a newborn king to see, our finest gifts we bring to lay before the king, so to honor him." And then he added his own: "Little baby, I am a poor boy too, I have no gift to bring that's fit to give our king. Shall I play for you?"

He took a deep breath, and while repeating the words in his mind, moved out of the shadows into the dim light. He swung the drum around to his belly, adjusted it and the leather strap to which it was attached, and then with a drumstick in each hand began drumming his gift to the King.

The sheep, lamb, and oxen began raising and lowering their front legs, keeping time with the music. Three well-dressed men stood next to the three saddled camels—the Magi, he knew—and all watched as he approached them.

Billy thought about closing his eyes, both embarrassed and hoping to hear the notes with greater intensity, but then the infant's mother held up her hand and nodded to him. *Mary,* he thought and wondered how he knew her name.

The infant King's eyes opened wide, and with tiny arms outstretched in Billy's direction, he smiled at him. Billy poured himself into the music, and as their eyes met, tears of joy began streaming down his little drummer boy's cheeks.

December 2019

CHAPTER 58

No Gold, Frankincense or Myrrh, Just a Dance

It's a cold, really cold, day during the holiday season, and at four-thirty in the afternoon, the screen on the weather station to my left indicates an outdoor temperature of minus four degrees and an indoor one of sixty-three degrees. It's dusk, and I'm doing my dance for fun and warmth while facing west into the forest. This view, regardless of the season, always intrigues and never disappoints me.

This late afternoon, I am not alone, as memories and the living surround me as I dance. In front of me, wedged up against the windowsill, is my great-grandfather's seaman's chest, the one he packed for the Atlantic crossings from Larvik, Norway to Brooklyn, New York, working journeys while he followed his star to a better life in America. It's an empty but beautiful chest, a relic now filled with memories and mythical stories—reminders of my ancestry.

Beyond the window of my second-story office, cautious, faintly perceptible four-legged creatures embracing the anonymity of semidarkness forage for food while following their own star. In the clearing, tree trunks like architects' slim, elegant writing tools rise above the cover of newly fallen snow amid thick "My First Ticonderoga #2" pencil-size pines.

There's a shape, a familiar yet foreign silhouette, in the woods. God, maybe? An incarnate presence or a lone white-tailed deer? It is Epiphany, Advent's over, and the Magi have been led to the baby Jesus. Whether in Spain, Italy, Bulgaria, Mexico, Australia, or the United States, people around the world are celebrating with parades of decorative floats. Jugglers juggle, and celebrants exchange gifts. Mountains and waters are blessed, while worshipping fools and revelers strip and plunge into icy rivers and lakes. Tasty breads and sweets are baked and shared, wines savored, and toasts made. The star which brought the three mysterious men to that particular manger on that specific night—the entire holy, mysterious, if not wonderfully crazy event—is celebrated.

My incongruous dance, uniquely mine, has no star to follow (or so I tell myself), no purpose other than to express my soul's yearnings, find joy, and bring contentment to my soul.

That's all I ask on this day of the Christmas season.

Tolstoy wrote:

> Everyone can feel God, but no one can truly understand God. Thus, do not attempt to understand God, but try instead to feel God's presence within you. If you are unable to find God there, then you will never find Him. When you look inside yourself, you see what is called "your own self" or your soul. You cannot touch it or see it or understand it, but you know it is there. And this part of yourself—that which you cannot understand—is what is called God. God is both around us and inside of us—in our souls.[1]

The dance continues, arms, legs, and body more synchronized and centered. The shapes and shadows beyond the windowpane are less distant than before, almost within reach. The incarnate one—or the lone deer—hasn't strayed, remaining erect and still, but now as my body persists in uninterrupted and unscripted movement, it has turned its head as if expecting another. And then there are two, now three, then four, and finally five apparitions emerging from the forest. I extend my left arm toward the window, wanting to touch and hug them, caress their heads, imagine holding out the blueberries and apple slices I extend to their mouths. Can they see my darkened form silhouetted against the hall light, or my shadow stretched across the ceiling? Do they mind or care?

Pope Francis, in a celebratory Epiphany mass, urged "... the faithful to be like the Magi, who, he said, continued to look at the sky, took risks and set out bearing gifts for Christ. If we want to find Jesus, we have to overcome our fear of taking risks, our self-satisfaction and our indolent refusal to ask anything more of life. We need to take risks simply to meet a child. Those risks are immensely worth the effort, since in finding that child, in discovering his tenderness and love, we rediscover ourselves."[2]

The reluctant disciple's dance, mine, is less frenetic than before, perhaps choreographed by the unknown and unknowing, but as I watch the parade of recognizable shapes, one following the other, walking slowly, light of foot, by the trees and into open space my dance is fearless, risky and assured.

Be still, my restless soul, and dance.

January 2018

CHAPTER 59

A Norwegian Christmas Greeting

Once upon a time I was bilingual—Norwegian was my second language. I've referenced those wonderful childhood years in Norway in previous posts, but I'm thinking of them today as Christmas approaches and friends and readers are in my thoughts. Though I'm no longer fluent in Norwegian, two words come to mind—*koselig* and *hyggelig,* words which defy adequate translation into English. Cozy comes close, but doesn't do them justice.

Christmas and the shortest day of the year are times when *koselig* and *hyggelig* describe how Norwegians feel while creating an atmosphere to keep the darkness and cold at bay. It is a palpable feeling of celebration and well-being.

Woolen caps, mittens, fur-lined coats and boots are gratefully discarded in the outer hallway. A bright blazing fire in the fireplace spreads warmth, and festive candlelight helps to set the tone of the evening. Hot chocolate, steaming coffee, tea, *gløgg,* red wine, and sparkling drinks facilitate the harmony of the moment. Meals, sumptuous entrées followed by tasty, colorful desserts and pastries are shared with family and friends. Spirited, fun-loving people gather, and a lyrical singsong of voices in conversation occurs while laughter echoes from room to room.

An enveloping sense of tranquility and belonging takes place, one in which friends and family feel safe and secure, as they leave the cold night air to relax in each other's presence.

With the warmth, contentment, and comfort of *koselig* and *hyggelig*, I wish you a joyful holiday and a Merry Christmas, or as Norwegians say, "*God Jul!*"

December 2016

CHAPTER 60

NEW YEAR, REALLY

What could I commit to doing in the coming year that would be sublimely foolish, out of character and foreign to my comfort zone, and yet be vigorously wholesome, insanely funny, and absurdly pleasure filled?

Dangerous territory, Roger, I think, while staring at the newly fallen snow outside my office window.

New Year's resolutions, when I succumb to the temptation to make them, have frustrated me and failed to bring change in my habits and lifestyle, and therefore, I avoid them. Even when they're well-intended and genuine, I rebel against them because I don't want to be denied, and being *told* to do anything, even when I'm the teller, is likely to meet with resistance—that's me. I do, however, want more joy and contentment, freshness and sparkle in my life in the coming year.

Quit this and embrace that, do less of this and more of that. My "this's and that's," the subjects for new resolve—exercise, food (chocolate excluded, yeah!) and drink, reading and writing, meditating and downtime, etc.—may be similar or different from yours, but we all have them or have thoughts of committing to them. They may all be worthy, but even so I end up, perhaps like you, dropping the resolutions, feeling disappointment, guilt, and a touch of relief, although not enough to sustain the stalwart pledge I'd made.

"No more!" I exclaim to no one in the forest beyond the window.

I look around as if someone might be listening—no one is—but I whisper anyway, "I'm going to dance every day of next year."

This is not about the cotillion, the cha cha, a rumba, merengue, tango, waltz, a Lindy Hop or a fine-tuned ballet technique. It *is* about movement—stepping, shuffling, shaking, bobbing and rolling, grunting, and sighing—and feeling my soul's music regardless of whether I'm on key or not. And if self-conscious inner chatter starts to drown out the tune, I'll sing, hum, or lip-sync my way back into the flow.

It could occur in an airport queue, a café while the barista makes my latte. It happens between the pews while parishioners recite the Prayer. I dance in front of the fire on Super Bowl Sunday, at Wrigley Field in the bottom of the ninth (Cubs down two but up to bat with no outs and men on second and third). I two-step with the Great Mystery between appointments in my office—spontaneous and freeing—anywhere and at any time, and therein lies the appeal and magic.

Is this a resolution? Yes and no. The former because it feels like great fun to me, and it's a commitment, and the latter because it lacks any smidgen of *should* or *ought*, the too frequent guilt-inducing underpinnings of my worthy goals.

I close my eyes and channel Fred Astaire's ceiling dance, John Travolta in *Grease* or *Pulp Fiction*, Patrick Swayze in *Dirty Dancing*, and Anthony Quinn in *Zorba the Greek*. Already I'm smiling.

And then the irrepressible James Brown appears center stage singing "Get On Up" as his boundless boogaloo energy lights up the room with mashed-potato and funky-chicken moves. I'm sold.

It's not a stretch for me to envision Jesus in full stride, working up a glorious sweat breakdancing to the cheers of his disciples and other wedding guests at the marriage in Cana, only to be interrupted when his mother grabs his robe and entreats him to do something. "The host has run out of wine!" she declares. The obedient but impatient son pulls off his first public miracle, and once the water in the six stone jars is transformed into the best wine, the carpenter from Nazareth acknowledges the applauding crowd of guests by resuming his athletic, eye-popping dance steps.

New Year beware, and as the old soul song goes, "Hold on, I'm comin'."

December 2017

ABOUT THE AUTHOR

ROGER MARUM is a psychotherapist of many years and also a religious and spiritual seeker. Faith, Doubt, and Listening: Lessons Learned by a Reluctant Disciple is his first book. Over the past dozen years, Roger has been writing about spiritual and psychological matters, both of which are his soul's passion, and muse.

He writes because he is filled with questions that concern and, at times, plague him: Does the practice of psychotherapy make a difference, and if so is that a function of methodology, personality, or the random connecting with a caring person? Is there a Higher Power, God, Divine Presence, or Supreme Creator—Alpha and Omega? Is there more to life than what his senses assimilate, and if so, how can one find even a restless peace in that "knowing?"

He is a reluctant disciple whose written words give voice to his questions, yearnings for truth, solace in times of despair and doubt, but most of all they make possible a deeper connection to the hope and resilience within him and all of us—a belief that starts with a risky leap of faith.

Roger received a PhD from Fuller Theological Seminary's Graduate School of Psychology and lives in Vermont. You can find him at https://www.yourreluctantdisciple.com/.

NOTES

Author's Note

1. Walter Winchell, In New York, *Naugatuck Daily News*, April 6, 1949, Page 4, Column 5, Naugatuck, Connecticut (Newspaper Archive)
   https://quoteinvestigator.com/2011/09/14/writing-bleed/

2. Paul Tillich, *Systematic Theology*, vol. 2 (Chicago: University of Chicago Press, 1975), 116–7.

Part 1

Chapter 2

1. Frederick Buechner, *Wishful Thinking: A Theological ABC* (New York: Harper & Row, 1973), 20.

Chapter 4

1. Thomas Fleet, *New England Primer*, 1st ed., 1737. To see an example of the original text, go to: https://english. hku.hk/staff/kjohnson/PDF/NewEnglandPrimerFORD1897. pdf and search on the word *sleep*.

Chapter 5

1. My mother was a poet and transposer of Scripture and ideas into verse that helped her, and she never cited where they came from. In this instance those days in the January readings triggered her writing soul. She wrote this verse without attribution to any text other than the *One Year Bible* and the words of the psalmist in Doris Marum's paraphrase (though some are identical words mixed with hers). Her verse is therefore an amalgamation of words from Psalm 25:1-22 in Doris Marum's version.

2. John Donne, "Meditation XVII," in *Devotions Upon Emergent Occasions,* (London: John W. Parker, 1839) 574–5, http://www.luminarium.org/sevenlit/donne/meditation17.php.

Part 2

Chapter 6

1. Maya Angelou (Maya Angelou@DrMayaAngelou), Twitter (quotation), May 23, 2014, 2:43 PM. https://twitter.com/DrMayaAngelou/status/469911477500272642

2. Maya Angelou, *I Know Why the Caged Bird Sings* (New York: Random House, 1969), 74.

Chapter 7

1. Reverend Martin Wheadon, "The Prayers of St. Teresa of Ávila," *Minister's Blog, Gants Hill URC,* April 17, 2020, https://www.gantshillurc.co.uk/ministers-blog/prayers-of-st-teresa-of-avila

Chapter 8

1. Toni Morrison, Nobel Prize speech, Stockholm, Sweden, December 10, 1993.

2. Bruno Bettelheim, *Freud and Man's Soul* (New York: Alfred A. Knopf, 1982), 110.

Chapter 10

1. Bettelheim, *Freud,* 110.

2. Martin Luther, "Defense and Explanation of All the Articles," in *Luther's Works,* vol. 32 *Career of the Reformer II,* ed. George W. Forell & Helmut T. Lehman (Fortress, 1958), 24.

3. Maya Angelou, "The Art of Fiction No 119," interview by George Plimpton, *Paris Review,* no.116 (Fall 1990), n.p.

4. Leonard Cohen, "Anthem," *The Future,* (Columbia Records, 1992).

Chapter 11

1. Ernest Hemingway, *Death in the Afternoon* (New York: Scribner, 1932), 153.

Chapter 12

1. Anne Lamott, *Plan B: Further Thoughts on Faith* (New York: Riverhead Books, 2005), 305.

Part 3

Chapter 13

1. Bettelheim, *Freud*, dust jacket.

Chapter 15

1. Debie Thomas, "Fumbling My Way into Prayer," *The Christian Century*, November 21, 2018, https://www.christiancentury.org/article/faith-matters/fumbling-my-way-contemplative-prayer

2. Henry David Thoreau, *The Essential Thoreau* (New York: Simon and Shuster, 2013) 532.

3. *The Oxford Dictionary of Quotations*, 2nd ed. (London: Oxford University press, 1953) 297.

4. Joseph Campbell, *Reflections on the Art of Living, A Joseph Campbell Companion* (New York: Harper Perennial, 1991), 18.

5. Frederick Buechner, *Telling Secrets: A Memoir* (New York: Harper One, 1991), 35.

6. L. Frank Baum, *Rinkitink in Oz* (Chicago: Reilly and Britton Co., 1916), chap. 1.

Chapter 16

1. Henri J. M. Nouwen, *Bread for the Journey: A Daybook of Wisdom and Faith* (New York: Harper Collins, 1997), n.p.

2. Frederick Buechner, *Listening to Your Life: Daily Meditations With Frederick Buechner* (New York: Harper Collins, 1992), 56.

3. Nouwen, *Bread for the Journey*.

Chapter 17

1. Mahatma Gandhi, *Gandhi, The Story of My Experiments with Truth, An Autobiography*, 1st ed. (Washington, DC: Public Affairs Press, 1948).

2. Buechner, *Wishful Thinking*, 53.

3. Ralph Greenson, *Loving, Hating, and Living Well : The Public Psychoanalytic Lectures of Ralph R. Greeson*, ed. Robert A. Nemiroff, Alan Sugarman, and Alvin Robbins (Madison: International Universities Press, 1992), 13.

Part 4

Chapter 18

1. Frederick Buechner, *Whistling in the Dark: A Doubter's Dictionary* (New York: Harper Collins, 1998), 44.

Chapter 21

1. Lloyd Cory, *Quote Unquote,* (Wheaton, IL: Victor Books, 1977) art 5.

Chapter 23

1. William James, *Principles of Psychology*, vol. 1, (New York: Dover Publications, Inc., 1950), 488.

Chapter 24

1. Ben Sisario, "Bob Dylan Speaks, At Last, On His Nobel," *New York Times*, October 28, 2016.

Chapter 26

1. Ralph Waldo Emerson, *Parnassus: An Anthology of Poetry*, edited by Ralph Waldo Emerson (Boston: Houghton, Osgood and Company, 1880) n.p.

2. Frederick Buechner, *Telling the Truth: The Gospel As Tragedy, Comedy, and Fairy Tale* (New York: Harper & Row, 1977), 33.

3. Paul Tillich, *The Eternal Now* (New York: Scribner, 1963), 2.

Chapter 29

1. Eleanor Roosevelt, "My Day," *United Features Syndicate*, March 6, 1940. Column can be viewed at: https://www2.gwu.edu/~erpapers/myday/displaydoc.cfm?_y=1940&_f=md055520.

Part 6

Chapter 30

1. Lawrence Wright, "Remembering Denis Johnson," *The New Yorker,* March 26, 2017.

2. David Marchese, "The Jazz Icon Sonny Rollins Knows Life Is A Solo Trip," *New York Times Magazine*, February 21, 2020.

3. William Shakespeare, *Henry VI, Part 2.* Act I, Scene 1, line 19; *The Complete Works of Shakespeare*, ed. Craig Hardin (Chicago: Scott Forsman & Co., 1961), 239.

Chapter 31

1. *Miles Davis Kind of Blue*, Columbia Records (recorded at Columbia Studios March 2nd and April 22, 1959, New York City).

2. .Buechner, *Telling the Truth*, 33.

3. Buechner, *Telling the Truth*, 33.

Chapter 32

1. Bill Doulos, "Join In Our Crusade," homily at Church of Our Saviour, San Gabriel, CA, November 27, 2016.

2. Nouwen, *Bread for the Journey.*

Chapter 33

1. Anne Lamott, *Hallelujah Anyway: Rediscovering Mercy* (New York: Riverhead Books, 2017), 10.

Part 7

Chapter 37

1. Jennifer Boudinot, *The Wit and Wisdom of Mark Twain* (New York: Chartwell Books, 2016).

2. Opie Read, *Mark Twain and I* (Chicago: Reilly & Lee Co., 1940), 34.

Chapter 38

1. Buechner, *Whistling in the Dark*, 82.

2. William James, *The Heart of William James*; ed. Robert Richardson (Cambridge & London: Harvard University Press, 2010), 219.

3. James, *Principles*, 369.

Chapter 39

1. Lawrence Wright, "Remembering Denis Johnson," *The New Yorker*, March 26, 2017.

2. Bettelheim, *Freud and Man's Soul*, 110.

Part 8

Chapter 41

1. Thomas Humphrey Ward, *The English Poets: Selections With Critical Introductions by Various Writers, and a General Introduction by Matthew Arnold; Edited by Thomas Humphrey Ward* (New York, London: Macmillan and Co., 2015) n.p.

2. William Hazlitt, *The Collected Works of William Hazlitt*, ed. A. R. Waller, Arnold Glover (London: J. M. Dent & Co.; New York: McClure Phillips & Co., 1903), 5. https://www.gutenberg.org/files/59506/59506-h/59506-h.htm

3. Mark Twain, "The Chronicle of Young Satan" (ca. 1897–1900, unfinished), published posthumously in Mark Twain's *Mysterious Stranger Manuscripts* (1969), ed. William Merriam Gibson, (Berkeley & Los Angeles: University of California Press, 2005), 165–166.

4 Leigh Hunt, *The Religion of the Heart: A Manual of Faith and Duty* (London: John Chapman, 1853), 62.

Chapter 42

1. Bettelheim, *Freud and Man's Soul*, 111.

2. Frederick Buechner, *Beyond Words* (New York: Harper Collins, 2004), 307.

Chapter 43

1. Louise Penny, *Still Life* (New York: Minotaur Books, 2005), 161.

Chapter 44

1. "Program Explores Universal Appeal of 'Amazing Grace,'" *The Washington Post*, August 25, 1990, https://www.washingtonpost.com/archive/local/1990/08/25/program-explores-universal-appeal-of-amazing-grace/13161fd2-a683-40ae-955e-2c8efea3bc38/.

Part 9

Chapter 46

1. James Lee Burke, *Jolie Blon's Bounce* (New York: Simon & Shuster, 2002), 345.

2. Burke, *Bounce*, 349.

3. Burke, *Bounce*, 349.

4. Burke, *Bounce*, 349.

Chapter 47

1. Rick Warren, *The Purpose-Driven Life* (Grand Rapids: Zondervan, 2002), 205.

Chapter 50

1. "Perry's Joint Café Puts Community First," *Pasadena Weekly*, June 18, 2020.

2. Ibid.

Chapter 52

1. J. R. R. Tolkien, *The Fellowship of the Ring* (London: Harper Collins, 1991), 222.

2. Tolkien, *Fellowship*, 222.

Part 10

Chapter 53

1. *Casablanca*, directed by Michael Curtiz, (1942; Burbank, CA: Warner Bros. Pictures).

2. Dietrich Bonhoffer, Sermon to German church in Barcelona on Sunday December 2, 1928.

Chapter 54

1 Frederick Buechner, *The Clown in the Belfry* (San Francisco: Harper Collins, 1992), 124.

2. Buechner, *Clown*, 124.

3. Buechner, *Clown*, 124.

4. Buechner, *Clown*, 124.

5. Buechner, *Clown*, 125.

Chapter 58

1. Leo Tolstoy, *Wise Thoughts for Every Day: On God, Love, Spirit, and Living a Good Life* (New York: Arcade Publishing, 2005), 4.

2 Pope Francis, "Like the Magi on Epiphany, Don't Be Afraid To Take Risks," (St. Peter's Basilica at the Vatican: Epiphany Mass) January 6, 2018.

www.ingramcontent.com/pod-product-compliance
Lightning Source LLC
Chambersburg PA
CBHW050338030726
47503CB00008B/2508